Gifts of God for the People of God

Exploring Worship in the Episcopal Church

Furman L. Buchanan

The scripture quotations contained herein are from The New Revised Standard Version Bible, copyright © 1989 by the Division of Christian Education of the National Council of the Churches of Christ in the U.S.A., and are used by permission. All rights reserved.

Psalm passages are from the Psalter in *The Book of Common Prayer*, unless otherwise noted.

0 Day of Peace, Words: Carl P. Daw, Jr. © 1982 Hope Publishing Company, Carol Stream, IL 60188. All rights reserved. Used by permission.

Author photo by Nill Silver

ISBN: 978-0-88028-466-0
© 2019 Forward Movement
All rights reserved.
Printed in the USA

Forward Movement
inspire disciples. empower evangelists.

Gifts of God for the People of God

Exploring Worship in the Episcopal Church

Furman L. Buchanan

Forward Movement
Cincinnati, Ohio

For Kim, Katherine, Finley, and Lamar,
four very special gifts from God in my life

Table of Contents

Preface

Discovering the Gifts

Many people arrive in the Episcopal Church—as I did years ago—unequipped to make sense of the worship experience. Visitors to my parish greet me after the service with facial expressions indicating they are glad they came, but they aren't sure what just happened. So much occurs in such a short period of time—standing, sitting, kneeling, and looking for the right page in *The Book of Common Prayer*. For someone new to liturgical worship, it takes one's full attention just to keep up. There is not much chance to ponder what we are doing and saying, or why.

I decided it would be helpful to develop a resource that explains what happens during a worship service along with an invitation for deeper reflection. In the Episcopal tradition, worship can take different forms, but this book will explore the service of Holy Eucharist—the service offered most often on Sunday mornings that includes the Liturgy of the Word (scriptures, sermon, praise, and prayers) and Holy Communion (the blessing and sharing of the Lord's Supper, sometimes described as the Liturgy of the Table). For clarity, the phrase Holy Eucharist (with capital H and E) refers to the entire worship service; eucharist or Holy Communion indicates the second part of the worship service. And communion (with a lower case c) describes the experience of oneness with God and others.

Through worship, we share an encounter with our living God. During these moments, God's story and our stories intersect as the gifts of God are celebrated and shared by the people of God.

In each chapter, we will explore a section of the service of Holy Eucharist: Rite Two. I have included the relevant sections from The Book of Common Prayer so it is easy to see how we move through the service and to be a visual reminder of the deeper meanings of each part of the liturgy.

I hope this book will help you discover the gifts of experiencing this holy communion with God. Gifts, after all, are meant to be opened and shared.

Chapter 1

Celebrating Communion

A Perfect Picture of God's Love

He is the image of the invisible God...

—Colossians 1:15

Imagine being invited to appear in a picture destined to become a classic image for the ages.

Imagine setting aside any qualms you may have about how you look. Imagine those concerns melting away with an assurance that the timeless quality of this picture does not depend upon you. You are simply invited to be a part of it.

Where would the picture be taken? What might you wear? Who would be in the picture with you? What makes the perfect picture?

For two-thousand years, the perfect picture of God's love is depicted by a simple meal among friends. The backdrop is a hidden room borrowed from a stranger. Jesus uses water to wash the feet of the disciples. Then he and his friends share a meal of bread and wine.

This picture is so perfect, so complete, that we re-imagine it every time we gather for the service of Holy Eucharist. When we come together for worship, we recall these first gifts of communion—of togetherness in the light of God's love, and we experience God's desire, through Christ, to be in communion with us.

Through the observance of the Holy Eucharist, the church carefully preserves and repeats the words and deeds of Jesus on that night. We also frame this perfect picture of God's love with other words and actions that prepare us to celebrate communion in Jesus' name and share his love with others. You do not have to imagine waiting for an invitation to receive these gifts of God, because God has already invited you. You do not have to imagine being invited to become part of the perfect picture of God's love, because you are already invited.

As an Episcopal priest, I have been privileged to celebrate the holy mysteries of God's love as revealed through the Holy Eucharist—in the bright light of day and in the darkness of a candlelight vigil. God's grace has shined through quiet celebrations with one other person and at noisy assemblies of hundreds. I have shared this simple, sacred meal with people for their first time and their last. We have celebrated with laughter and with tears.

The gifts imparted through the sharing of the Holy Eucharist are as innumerable as the masses of people who have been nourished by this sacrament from every tribe, language, people, and nation for two-thousand years. You would surely describe your experiences of these gifts differently. This is as it should be, because we all follow different journeys to and from this celebration of God's love.

What we have in common (and in communion) is the all-embracing love of God revealed in the story of Jesus Christ. What we hold in particular is our own stories along life's pathways.

Holy Eucharist is where God's common love story and our particular stories intersect. As surely as the Bible is the testament of God's love, Holy Eucharist is the means by which we consume that love so that it becomes an indistinguishable part of our own souls and bodies. Worship is a gift that sustains us as we appear in the next chapter of God's love story.

I want to take you on a journey through the worship service of Holy Eucharist as we celebrate it in the Episcopal Church using *The Book of Common Prayer*. Even if you are from another tradition in the church, you will recognize most, if not all, of these elements.

Beginning with the opening words and following through to the final dismissal, I invite you to discover some of the special gifts of God. I will try to open up these gifts through stories—biblical and personal. They help point to some of the surprising ways God's love is communicated to us when we worship, and then through us when we love our neighbors as ourselves. Ultimately, I hope these stories challenge and inspire you to reflect upon your own particular stories that shape the way you encounter the gifts of communion with God and your neighbor.

As we begin our reflection on Holy Eucharist and the stories that bind us, one to another and all to Christ, I will share with you a tale that I believe offers a picture of what life with God and one another is supposed to look like.

One of my favorite photographs from my childhood features a passel of boys and girls clinging to eight steps on a ladder that ascends to a brand-new treehouse. Freshly cut pine boards shine like golden halos over the heads of happy children. The only thing missing was some of our teeth. But when you're eight years old, you don't let missing teeth stand in the way of big smiles when you experience a great gift.

If I were making up a parable about the joy and wonder of experiencing the gift of love, it would start like this: "Once upon a time, a father built a tree house for his son. He made it tall enough for the boy to see the world from a new perspective. He erected walls and a roof to make it safe and dry enough for sleeping under the stars. Most importantly, he let his son help build it in order to show that perfection is not necessary for goodness. It was a gift of love, one that lasts a lifetime."

How does your parable about love begin? What is your favorite picture of receiving a gift that was more than you deserved?

Near the end of the New Testament is a letter to the Hebrews. This letter begins with another picture of how God's love story has developed over time. The writer explains that while God used to speak to our ancestors through prophets, there is a new means of revelation for us now—a Son who reflects God's glory, a Son who is the exact imprint of God's very being!

Think about that for a moment. God's people used to have the words of the Law and the prophets but now also have the picture of Jesus. As the letter to the Colossians also says, "He is the image of the invisible God" (1:15).

It is as if the invisible source of light and life, mysteriously present in all things, used the light of divine countenance to take a picture that captures the truth and beauty of love in a human face. It is as if God shared a favorite picture of a gift that was more than any of us deserved.

Scripture contains numerous theological metaphors related to photography that the ancient writers could not have known. I wouldn't know the significance of these metaphors without the help of my daughter, who shared with me what she learned from a photography class.

It turns out that a brief exposure to light is all that is necessary to create an image. That's all a camera does—it simply lets a little light shine in. What a wonderful metaphor for what we do when we celebrate Holy Eucharist! We take the time to be still long enough to experience the perfect image of God's love and let a little of that light shine in.

And yet, while light is necessary to create an image, the photograph requires darkness to develop. Jesus—the imprint of God's being—suffered in the darkness of human cruelty as the full portrait of God's love came into focus. We have been given the courage to persevere in our own valleys of darkness by seeing more clearly that God does not do bad things to us. Rather, our God suffers bad things with us.

After the picture develops in the dark, then we bring it back into the light to view the full image with all of its subtleties. Through the stories of scripture, we are blessed with many pictures of Jesus sharing the love of God, welcoming children and adults into his arms and blessing them. In our own snapshots too, we see God's love, in big ways and in small, from the knots in golden pine boards to gaps between the teeth of children's smiles. In all these images, we have the gift of joy and wonder in seeing God's love.

During the service of Holy Eucharist, we are invited to take and develop our own pictures of God's love. We open our minds to let God's light shine in. We also gain strength and courage to persevere in the dark, trusting that God is there with us, too. Ultimately, we receive the joy and wonder of God's love, imprinted on our own hearts in living color.

What's even more incredible is that the picture of Jesus—the exact imprint of God—is not for our benefit only. I believe this image is also a blessing for God. This new understanding came to me as I realized that while my father built the tree house for me, he took the picture for himself.

As a father, I can understand why God the Father built an entire kingdom for his children. God did so to delight in those glorious smiles—toothless or not. God does this to give us more inquiring hearts, more courageous spirits, and more joy and wonder in it all.

In the Holy Eucharist, we join a celebration in which our picture counts. Our presence makes a difference in the picture—as a blessing to God the Almighty and a blessing to our sisters and brothers and to our neighbors.

Whether the light is shining or the darkness surrounds us, we are making a family photo album one page at a time. And Jesus is the perfect picture for the cover. These pages of the scrapbook are meant to be filled with images and stories of this love as we have received and shared it with one another.

When we celebrate the Holy Eucharist, we are giving thanks for God's desire to be in communion with us, no matter what. We also are celebrating a perfect picture of God's love and our place in that picture, here and now. Our presence in that picture gladdens the very heart of God, for it is the image of our thanksgiving—our eucharist—and it is holy.

Reflecting on Our Story with God

❖ Look through a photo album or browse pictures on your telephone or computer. How do these pictures illustrate the gift of God's love communicated through and with other people?

❖ Reflect on celebrations of Holy Eucharist that have been especially meaningful and memorable.

Celebrating Our Story with God

❖ Copy or re-photograph some of your favorite "pictures" of the love of God communicated through the gifts, graces, and mercies of other people.

❖ Offer thanks to God for these people, experiences, and memories.

❖ If possible, write a note of gratitude (including a copy of the picture) to people who appear in one of these pictures, letting them know how they are part of one of your favorite images of God's love.

Chapter 2

Jesus Is Coming

The First as well as the Last Supper

Blessed is the one who comes in the name of the Lord.

—*Psalm 118:26*

The pattern of the liturgy for Holy Eucharist is derived not only from the Last Supper Jesus shares with his disciples before his death but also from the first supper he shares with his disciples after his resurrection. Holy Eucharist unfolds like a two-act drama, patterned after the resurrection story of Jesus' secret walk to Emmaus with two of his disciples and their meal together.

In *The Book of Common Prayer*, the major "acts" in the liturgy for Holy Eucharist help make this clear. The first headline is "The Word of God." This corresponds with the hearing and remembering part of our worship. The second headline, "The Holy Communion," corresponds with the sacred meal part of our worship. If we were to look at the first supper story from Chapter 24, verses 13-35, of Saint Luke's Gospel in light of these two acts, it would look like this:

The Word of God

Now on the same day, two of [Jesus' disciples] were going to a village called Emmaus, about seven miles from Jerusalem, and talking with each other about all these things that had happened. While they were talking and discussing, Jesus himself came near and went with them, but their eyes were kept from recognizing him. And he said to them, "What are you discussing with each other while you walk along?" They stood still, looking sad. Then one of them, whose name was Cleopas, answered him, "Are you the only stranger in Jerusalem who does not know the things that have taken place there in these days?" He asked them, "What things?" They replied, "The things about Jesus of Nazareth, who was a prophet mighty in deed and word before God and all the people, and how our chief priests and leaders handed him over to be condemned to death and crucified him. But we had hoped that he was the one to redeem Israel. Yes, and besides all this, it is now the third day since these things took place. Moreover, some women of our group astounded us. They were at the tomb early this morning, and when they did not find his body there, they came back and told us that they had indeed seen a vision of angels who said that he was alive. Some of those who were with us went to the tomb and found it just as the women had said; but they did not see him." Then he said to them, "Oh, how foolish you are, and how slow of heart to believe all that the prophets have declared! Was it not necessary that the Messiah should suffer these things and then enter into his glory?" Then beginning with Moses and all the prophets, he interpreted to them the things about himself in all the scriptures.

The Holy Communion

As they came near the village to which they were going, he walked ahead as if he were going on. But they urged him strongly, saying, "Stay with us, because it is almost evening and the day is now nearly over." So he went in to stay with them. When he was at the table with them, he took bread, blessed and broke it, and gave it to them. Then their eyes were opened, and they recognized him; and he vanished from their sight. They said to each other, "Were not our hearts burning within us while he was talking to us on the road, while he was opening the scriptures to us?" That same hour they got up and returned to Jerusalem; and they found the eleven and their companions gathered together. They were saying, "The Lord has risen indeed, and he has appeared to Simon!" Then they told what had happened on the road, and how he had been made known to them in the breaking of the bread.

†

Every now and then, I see a bumper sticker that always makes me smile. It reads, "Jesus is coming. Look busy!"

This reminds me of a common experience in elementary school: The teacher steps out of the classroom for a moment and utter bedlam unfolds—at the chalkboard, at student's desks, *on* student's desks. A fellow student serves as scout, peeking through a crack in the door.

And then the inevitable, "Here she comes!" Fear surges in our stomachs as we scurry to get seated, open books, pick up pencils, all to give the appearance of being busy.

In Luke's story of Jesus meeting two disciples on the road to Emmaus, we have the teacher—Rabbi—who (to say the least) has been detained by some other work for three days. But these followers haven't been on the lookout. Instead, they are reeling in sadness. Their hope that maybe, just maybe, Jesus would redeem Israel has been dashed when he died an ignoble death on the cross.

They are not expecting Jesus. They have no reason to look busy. In fact, they are doing their best to try to sort out the confusion of the last few days. They ask in disbelief, *Are you the only stranger in town who doesn't know what has been going on?*

Using our modern, colloquial expression, Cleopas might just as easily express his astonishment with the question, *Have you been in a cave?* Which, of course, Jesus has.

Like so many times before, Jesus turns the expected on its head. The disciples actually begin to describe who Jesus was as a prophet to Jesus the Prophet. How embarrassing!

The disciples have let fear, hurt, and anxiety cloud their judgment, and they forget the words of the prophets. Jesus sets out to work on their "mental clutter"—Luke tells us that "beginning with Moses and *all the prophets,*" Jesus gives a good, solid lesson as they walk along. Imagine what it would feel like to be on the receiving end of that lecture!

Despite the suffering, death, and resurrection, at least some among the inner circle are ready to chalk Jesus up as another dead prophet. Yet, their hearts burn as they listen to some of the most inspiring teaching of their lives. So, they invite this stranger to dinner. And—thanks be to God—he accepts their invitation.

So, maybe the bumper sticker *should* read, "Jesus is coming. Invite a stranger to dinner!" Don't *look* busy; just share your bread with a stranger or a friend. The lesson about Jesus and the disciples at the table in Emmaus shows that those two types of dinner guests are really one and the same—the stranger turns out to be the friend.

This is the cornerstone of Christian hospitality—the expectation that we will meet Christ in the stranger. Remember Jesus' admonition in the Gospel according to Matthew: "Just as you did it to the least of these who are members of my family, you did it to me" (25:40). Or in the Letter to the Hebrews: "Do not neglect to show hospitality to strangers, for by doing that some have entertained angels without knowing it" (13:2).

We also find this emphasis on hospitality in the Acts of the Apostles in which the earliest believers were described as devoted "to the apostles' teaching and fellowship, the breaking of the bread and the prayers"(2:42). This pattern of faithful living, half of which is concerned with fellowship and breaking bread, is so critical that it is one of our baptismal promises. During the sacrament of Holy Baptism, we are asked, "Will *you* continue in the apostle's teaching and fellowship, in the breaking of the bread and in the prayers?"

When we invite strangers and friends to dinner, we honor our baptismal vows. When we share hospitality with strangers among us, we honor our baptismal vows.

Being faithful is not about looking busy—or even *being* busy. Being faithful is about breaking bread with one another and with our Lord—a Lord who sneaks up on us in places where food is found, like a feeding trough in a run-down, Bethlehem barn or a grand outdoor picnic of bread and fish along the seashore or a Last Supper in a discreet, upper room.

Even now, our Lord sneaks up on us, is present with us, when we share with those who are hungry or serve meals to those in need. Jesus is with us when we show hospitality to strangers and to friends—and when we receive hospitality from strangers and friends.

Most of all, our Lord is known to us when we show up for the Holy Eucharist. Interestingly, our worship reflects the pattern of that day on the way to Emmaus. We begin with the Liturgy of the Word, hearing from the prophets and listening to the gospel so that we might better recognize Christ and better understand his glorious ministry.

Then, whether or not we understand all the prophets and teachings, we invite Jesus to our table as we offer gifts of bread and wine. Just like that evening in Emmaus, Christ says yes to our invitation. We gather around the table—some of us friends and some of us strangers—and we receive Christ, right there in the bread and wine.

And here's the profound and remarkable twist: Christ receives us! It doesn't matter if we are like Cleopas or the other disciple, foolish or failing to recognize Jesus in our midst. It doesn't matter if we are like the disciples, bereft and hopeless. None of that matters.

That's because our Lord is the one who takes, blesses, breaks, and shares what he has—his bread and even his precious life—for the health and salvation of his disciples. Our Lord is committed to giving us what we need and cannot give ourselves.

Anglican priest and hymn writer George Wallace Briggs articulated the request of the disciples at Emmaus. It is a prayer that invites Jesus—and recognizes the fact that Jesus really invites us to the table. "Come risen Lord, and deign to be our guest; nay, let us be thy guests; the feast is thine; thyself at thine own board make manifest in thine own Sacrament of Bread and Wine" (*The Hymnal 1982*, #305).

In other words, Jesus is coming. Let's have dinner!

Reflecting on Our Story with God

❖ Try to remember an occasion when you felt surprised by the presence of God, particularly when you could not see (or refused to see) God's grace initially.

❖ Reflect on an occasion when you reached out to a stranger and experienced a blessing.

❖ Think of a time when the Liturgy of the Word did not make sense but you accepted the invitation to Christ's table anyway.

Celebrating Our Story with God

❖ Consider how your worship and service in Jesus' name is based not only on the memory of the Last Supper but also upon the hope and expectation of the First Supper.

❖ Explore new ways to give, serve, share, and receive food as part of your life of faith.

❖ Jesus is coming. Imagine how to both look and be less busy in order to make time to encounter him more deeply.

The Word
of the Lord

Chapter 3

Blessed Be God & God's Kingdom

First Things First

In the beginning was the Word, and the Word was with God, and the Word was God.

—John 1:1

Blessed—the very first word spoken during the worship service of Holy Eucharist —tells us everything we need to know. The purpose of worship is, after all, to bless God. Of course, we come to church for lots of reasons: to be part of a community, to visit with friends, to hear an excellent sermon and stirring music. But the first word of the service reminds us of this important fact: Our worship is not about us. It is about blessing God.

The term "Holy Eucharist" itself offers additional insight into what we are doing when we gather for worship. "Holy" means

The Holy Eucharist: Rite Two

The Word of God

A hymn, psalm, or anthem may be sung.

The people standing, the Celebrant says

Blessed be God: Father, Son, and Holy Spirit.

People   And blessed be his kingdom, now and for ever. Amen.

In place of the above, from Easter Day through the Day of Pentecost

Celebrant   Alleluia. Christ is risen.
People   The Lord is risen indeed. Alleluia.

In Lent and on other penitential occasions

Celebrant   Bless the Lord who forgives all our sins.
People   His mercy endures for ever.

The Celebrant may say

Almighty God, to you all hearts are open, all desires known, and from you no secrets are hid: Cleanse the thoughts of our hearts by the inspiration of your Holy Spirit, that we may perfectly love you, and worthily magnify your holy Name; through Christ our Lord. *Amen.*

—The service for Holy Communion begins on page 355 of *The Book of Common Prayer.*

"set apart" or "special." And *eucharistia* is the Greek word for "thanksgiving." Therefore, the service of Holy Eucharist is our act of offering a special thanksgiving to God for all the blessings we have received. So it is logical that the very first word we use to describe the One from whom all blessings flow is "blessed."

In a fitting symmetry, one of the last words spoken in the liturgy is also "bless." At the end of the Holy Eucharist, the deacon dismisses the people into the world to serve others in God's name.

One of the dismissal statements is: "Let us bless the Lord." This statement recognizes two fundamental ways to bless the Lord—one way is through prayer and worship when we gather; the other way is by loving our neighbors as ourselves when we are dismissed.

In the Episcopal Church, the priest is the one who calls people to gather in the Lord's name, and the deacon dismisses the people to serve in the Lord's name. Worship and service are two sides of the same coin—they are both indispensable acts of faith as we have come to understand faith through the example of Jesus Christ.

In the first act of Holy Eucharist—the Word of God—blessing is made incarnate through prayer. We offer prayers of praise and adoration. After listening to the story of God and affirming this story in the words of the Nicene Creed, we offer our prayers of thanksgiving and intercession. Next, we offer prayers of confession. And finally, after being reconciled with God and one another, we offer our prayer of oblation—giving ourselves, the fruit of our souls and bodies, to the glory of God.

Thus, the Word of God portion of the Holy Eucharist involves far more than passive listening to biblical readings and a sermon; it is an engaged, active response by all the people to God's love.

In short, we are praying—by word and deed—to a God who is worthy of blessing, while we are responding—by word and deed—to the blessing of God's kingdom on earth as it is in heaven. Throughout this portion of the service, as we move through the prayers and responses, it is important to remember that they all flow from the very first word: blessed.

And not only blessed be God, but blessed be God's kingdom. But what is God's kingdom? What do we mean by this phrase? I believe the kingdom of God is not a place in the way we normally think of an earthly kingdom as having a specific geographic location. When Jesus talks about the kingdom of God, he often compares it with a thing or even describes it as a verb. Examples include *sowing* seeds, *mixing* yeast, *hiding* treasure, and *finding* a great pearl (Matthew 13).

Jesus encourages us to see the kingdom of God as an invitation, a celebration, and a journey. This blessed kingdom can also entail judgment, as found in Jesus' Parable of the Bridesmaids in Saint Matthew's Gospel.

> Jesus said, "Then the kingdom of heaven will be like this. Ten bridesmaids took their lamps and went to meet the bridegroom. Five of them were foolish, and five were wise. When the foolish took their lamps, they took no oil with them; but the wise took flasks of oil with their lamps. As the bridegroom was delayed, all of them became drowsy and slept. But at midnight there was a shout, 'Look! Here is the bridegroom! Come out to meet him.' Then all those bridesmaids got up and

trimmed their lamps. The foolish said to the wise, 'Give us some of your oil, for our lamps are going out.' But the wise replied, 'No! there will not be enough for you and for us; you had better go to the dealers and buy some for yourselves.' And while they went to buy it, the bridegroom came, and those who were ready went with him into the wedding banquet; and the door was shut. Later the other bridesmaids came also, saying, 'Lord, lord, open to us.' But he replied, 'Truly I tell you, I do not know you.' Keep awake therefore, for you know neither the day nor the hour."

—Matthew 25:1-13

†

Most of us can remember special moments of celebration in our lives when our families and friends—sometimes even people we don't know—have gathered with us to mark a special occasion: baptisms, weddings, birthdays and anniversaries, sports banquets, recitals, graduations, and even funerals. These occasions can offer us glimpses of the blessed kingdom.

One of the kingdom moments in my life took place early in the morning on a cool September day at the Opening Convocation of Wofford College in 1987. This convocation was in the auditorium of the historic "Old Main" building, which stands at the center of the campus. The gravity of this 133-year tradition was perceptible to everyone in the room.

A convocation is a ceremonial assembly when college and university presidents call together their faculty, dressed in full academic regalia, and their students, preferably dressed with some respectability. These events celebrate the beginning of a new school year. It is an opportunity for the president to recognize and welcome new professors and students. The academic dean encourages everyone to study diligently, explore new ideas, and meet new challenges.

At this convocation there was one other item on the program, immediately following the president's opening welcome. Dr. Joe Lesesne was going to publicly name me as the new presidential scholar, a student selected for the privilege and responsibility of spending the upcoming year traveling independently around the world.

I felt deeply honored to be considered worthy for an invitation to such an invaluable, life-changing opportunity. The kingdom of heaven is like this: an invitation to an invaluable, life-changing opportunity.

I was also overwhelmed and scared by the idea of embarking on a solo journey to foreign places, cut off from familiar faces and voices. The kingdom of heaven is also like this: a journey upon which we embark to an unfamiliar reality we cannot control.

Yet despite my fears, I was proud to be commissioned and sent forth by the president of the college and to receive the blessing and support of my professors and fellow students. There is nothing quite like receiving the blessing of people you admire and love. The kingdom of heaven is also like this: a celebration overflowing with blessings beyond what we deserve.

The grand, antique bell in one of the twin towers of Old Main began to toll the hour, and the faculty in their gowns and academic hoods formed a processional line behind the dean to ascend the twenty-eight steps that framed the historic building like an apron. The students in the auditorium stood respectfully as the procession entered from the back of the room. The president, the dean, and the college chaplain stepped onto the stage while the faculty gradually filled in the first rows of seats.

I could not *see* this procession from where I was, but I could *hear* the toll of the bell. Thank God, I could hear the bell! You see, I was sound asleep in my dormitory. Jesus said, "Keep awake therefore, for you know neither the day nor the hour."

The numbers on my digital alarm clock reported with precision the shocking judgment of my dilemma. I don't know what happened to the alarm on my clock, but the alarm gripping me from inside was dreadful. The kingdom of heaven is like this too: a celebration that happens—*with* us or *without* us.

Under these circumstances, one quickly distinguishes the essential from the merely important. It is essential that one wear clothes to an opening convocation, but it is merely important for those clothes to match. It is essential to brush one's teeth before leaving for such an auspicious occasion, but it is merely important to brush one's hair. The kingdom of heaven is like this: a reality that compels us to distinguish between what is essential and what is merely important.

I ran as fast as I could down the sidewalk toward Old Main, and I learned on that morning that it is possible to run and tie a half Windsor knot in a necktie at the same time.

I attacked the steps three at a time. I ripped open the door, ran my hands through my hair, and slipped into the back of the auditorium at the precise moment the president called out my name. The kingdom of heaven is like this: We are called by our names whether we are listening or not.

I walked to the stage to receive a framed certificate as an outward and visible sign of this scholarship. The text of the certificate included adjectives like "responsible, diligent, and conscientious." Conspicuously missing were words *more* descriptive of me on that particular morning, like "careless, foolish, and unprepared."

Perhaps some of the people interpreted my breathlessness as excitement or nervousness. And, ironically, their interpretation was right. I was excited and nervous for good reasons and for not-so-good reasons. The kingdom of heaven is like this: We are recognized by grace for merits we have not earned, and we are mercifully forgiven for flaws we simply cannot deny.

All throughout the gospels, Jesus repeatedly tells people that the kingdom of God has come near. He urges them to pay attention to what is right under their noses. Why should we expect God's kingdom to be any different in our day and time?

The kingdom has always been introduced with a call. Indeed, the original word for church—*ekklesia*—is based upon the ancient Greek word for "call." It literally means "called out"—called out of nowhere, like a bell ringing faintly in the distance, called out of familiar comforts to embark on a new journey, called out of slumber to join a celebration.

The kingdom is much nearer, more diverse, and surprising than we can imagine. Our personal answers to kingdom invitations, journeys, and celebrations may take time and prayer in order to emerge more clearly.

But there is no better place to start searching for glimpses of our own blessed kingdom responses than in the very place where we worship the Lord of this kingdom. It is the place where we pray as he taught us to pray—for God's kingdom to come here and God's will to be done now.

So we must keep awake, therefore, for we know neither the day nor the hour when our prayers will be answered and we will experience God's here-and-now kingdom. We must keep awake, therefore, to hear God's invitation, join the celebration, and embark on our journey.

Reflecting on Our Story with God

❖ When you think about why you attend worship, is blessing God the most important reason? How might this perspective change your attitude, preparation, and participation in worship?

❖ The kingdom has always been an invitation to a life-changing opportunity, and other faithful people have accepted this invitation and passed it down to us. What life-changing invitations have you received to experience God's blessed kingdom?

❖ The kingdom has always been a journey into an unfamiliar reality. Many faithful people have embarked on this bold and new journey with Jesus—and without expertise. What journeys into unfamiliar territory have you taken that led to blessings of new discovery and promise?

❖ The kingdom has always been a celebration overflowing with blessings, and other faithful people have shared these sacraments for two millennia and passed them on to us. At which important celebrations have you experienced blessings and mercies?

Celebrating Our Story with God

❖ What new, specific words and deeds—in worship and in service to others—might you try out in order to exemplify "blessed be God and God's kingdom," which we express at the beginning and the end of the service of Holy Eucharist?

❖ What invitations might you extend to others so they will experience the blessed kingdom?

❖ What journeys might you help lead with other pilgrims who are seeking and serving Christ in the blessed kingdom?

❖ What celebrations might you host or help sponsor that would bestow blessings and mercies upon others?

Chapter 4

Gloria in excelsis

Adoption for Good

And suddenly there was with the angel a multitude of the heavenly host, praising God and saying, "Glory to God in the highest heaven, and on earth peace among those whom he favors!"

—Luke 2:13-14

Whereas the first word—and purpose—in the service of Holy Eucharist is to bless God and God's kingdom, the first means of blessing God is through a song of praise. We most often sing a song we learned from the angels the night Jesus was born.

Gloria in excelsis is the Latin name for a song that proclaims, "Glory to God in the highest heaven, and on earth peace..." Singing *Gloria in excelsis* reminds us that our Father's glory in heaven also shines through the peace his only begotten Son brought to earth.

When appointed, the following hymn or some other song of praise is sung or said, all standing

Glory to God in the highest,
    and peace to his people on earth.

Lord God, heavenly King,
almighty God and Father,
        we worship you, we give you thanks,
        we praise you for your glory.

Lord Jesus Christ, only Son of the Father,
Lord God, Lamb of God,
you take away the sin of the world:
        have mercy on us;
you are seated at the right hand of the Father:
        receive our prayer.

For you alone are the Holy One,
you alone are the Lord,
you alone are the Most High,
        Jesus Christ,
        with the Holy Spirit,
        in the glory of God the Father. Amen.

On other occasions the following is used

Lord, have mercy.		Kyrie eleison.
Christ, have mercy.	*or*	*Christe eleison.*
Lord, have mercy.		Kyrie eleison.

or this

Holy God,
Holy and Mighty,
Holy Immortal One,
Have mercy upon us.

The Collect of the Day

The Celebrant says to the people

The Lord be with you.

People   And also with you.

Celebrant   Let us pray.

The Celebrant says the Collect.

People   Amen.

—The service for Holy Communion continues on page 356 of *The Book of Common Prayer.*

In fact, Jesus reveals the full glory of God fleshed out. Through Jesus, we observe how peace and other divine virtues are practiced by a real human being in a real human family. Jesus shows us all of the virtues available to the children of God.

Yet, there is more going on in this song of praise than just seeing God's glory as a bystander or wishing for peace on earth as a passive observer. When the angels sing *Gloria in excelsis* on Christmas night, they celebrate God and humanity, heaven and earth, birth and adoption, miraculously bound together as one.

On Christmas night, the Divine Family and the human family become blended for good. The angels sing because Jesus is born and also because the human family is adopted by the love of God through the unbreakable love between a Father and his only begotten Son.

In a similar way, we blend our voices to sing of God's glory, not as passive observers but as direct beneficiaries of Jesus' birth into the human family and consequently, our adoption into the family of God. If God and God's kingdom are as blessed as we say when we begin our worship, then the *Gloria in excelsis* is our opportunity to express praise and thanksgiving that God was willing to become a living member of the human family and deem us worthy to become members of the Divine Family. When we sing (or speak) this song, we are responding with awe and gratitude that God believes in blended families for goodness's sake.

✝

My family intimately understands the priceless gift of adoption. This gift inspired my grandmother to sing glory to God. Yet, our story begins not with a joyful birth but with a tragic and untimely death. It begins like the story of Lazarus from the Gospel according to Saint John.

> [Mary] knelt at [Jesus'] feet and said to him, "Lord, if you had been here, my brother would not have died." When Jesus saw her weeping, and the Jews who came with her also weeping, he was greatly disturbed in spirit and deeply moved. He said, "Where have you laid him?" They said to him, "Lord, come and see." Jesus began to weep. So the Jews said, "See how he loved him!" But some of them said, "Could not he who opened the eyes of the blind man have kept this man from dying?"
>
> —John 11:32-27

At the center of the story is a young woman who reflects both Mary and Martha. Like Martha, this woman knew her way around the kitchen and was not afraid of hard work. She wanted things to be just right for special guests, like having a piping hot, freshly baked peach pie on the kitchen counter.

And like Mary, on at least one dark night—and perhaps many—this 27-year-old mother of three young boys cried out to Jesus, "Lord, if you had been here, my husband would not have died."

Mary and Martha needed Jesus to show up sooner—and with a healing miracle to save their brother, Lazarus. Their story is also *our* story. We need Jesus to show up with a healing miracle for us and those we love. And sometimes we are disappointed. Sometimes we are left with bitter grief when there are no miracles and people who we love die.

In the midst of the Great Depression, with life insurance a luxury and Social Security a distant dream, Carrie Lee Buchanan, peach-pie baker and my grandmother, was widowed. She was left with three young boys, the sting of her husband's death, and not much else.

Some of the family urged Carrie Lee to send her boys to an orphanage. After all, the economy was in shambles. There was no way she could eke out a living without a husband or a job and three children, ages five, three, and one.

Carrie Lee was facing an impossible choice until her sister, brother-in-law, and their young children invited them into their home. But they did not just welcome Carrie Lee and her boys into their home until the shock of death wore off or until she could find a suitable orphanage. They adopted them into their home for good. They were all adopted into that family for life.

My father and his brothers regarded their uncle (and aunt) as the greatest people who ever walked the face of the earth—save for Jesus Christ. The reason they could say that and mean it was because for them, Uncle Linwood was the personification of Jesus.

Their uncle showed up with a miracle when all hope was gone. Their uncle offered hope in the midst of fears of being shipped to an orphanage and being separated from their family. Their uncle showed up with the promise of a new life—and not just any new life but one lived together as a family. It is no wonder my father and his brothers praised his name.

We are called to personify Jesus in a broken world. As the church, we are called to be the Body of Christ in the midst of hopelessness, despair, and grief.

Sometimes that means opening our homes. Sometimes it means opening our hearts. Other times, personifying Jesus just means opening our arms and embracing others through Christ's love. We are inspired to sing God's praises for our adoption into the Divine Family, even as we are inspired to practice these same, loving virtues here on earth.

Our Lord Jesus Christ comes to us in our grief and weeps with us. He comes to us through the grace and love of real human homes, real human hearts, and real human arms. Our Lord Jesus Christ brings us new life—not just when we die, but here and now through the miracles we give and receive in his name.

And just like the resurrection of new life that Carrie Lee and her sons experienced through their adoption, our Lord Jesus Christ still graciously adopts us into his home—not for a season but for good.

Most of us will not be faced with the situation of adopting a young widow and her three children. But we are faced with opportunities to "adopt" every day. Social surveys show that one in three young adults claim no religious affiliation. Many church leaders are wringing their hands over these statistics, wondering how to reverse the decline. I think the answer is simple: We need to reach forth our hands in love. We need to adopt those who could use a little more grace and love in their lives—and that includes everybody, doesn't it?

This might not seem completely reasonable or realistic, but Jesus doesn't spend a lot of energy on showing us how to be reasonable. Reasonable people send impossible problems to orphanages. Jesus shows us how to be resurrection people, and resurrection people say, "You are welcome in our house, not just for a season but for good!" Resurrection people say, "We will make sacrifices for you to be included here." Resurrection people say, "We will do whatever it takes for the sake of Christ's love because it is only by Christ's love that we found our home here."

A church that practices adoption begins to look like the vision of Saint John the Divine in the Book of Revelation: "See! The home of God is among mortals. He will dwell with them; they will be his peoples, and God himself will be with them" (21:3).

This practice of adoption into the Divine Family promises new life, bound together with Christ and one another in the household of God. It's a big house. It's often unwieldy and chaotic, with plenty of chores. Yet, it is a house filled with songs of God's praise and wonders of God's love.

Just like that very first night long ago when the angels joined with the heavenly host to sing "Glory to God in the highest heaven and peace on earth," we sing God's praise, not only with our lips but in our lives. We praise God with every fiber of our being because we have been welcomed into the Divine Family, and we also praise God by welcoming others in Jesus' name—not just for a season but for good!

Reflecting on Our Story with God

❖ Try to remember a time you were adopted (or chosen)—literally or figuratively—by a family, a friend, a community, a team, or some other group.

❖ Imagine Christmas not only as the birth of God's Son into a human family but also as the adoption of the human family into God's household. How might this enlarge our sense of belonging to God's family?

❖ If we were to consider ourselves as fully part of a divinely blended family, how might that inspire us to seek more peace with our sisters and brothers?

Celebrating Our Story with God

❖ Consider how you might open your heart, your arms, or your home to someone who needs to experience God's love.

❖ Consider writing a song in your own words that praises God's glory in heaven and celebrates God's peace on earth.

Chapter 5

The Lessons

Listen Up!

They heard the sound of the Lord God walking in the garden.

—*Genesis 3:8*

After we offer our praise to God, we sit and listen to the story of God and what life with God is like through readings from the Old Testament, the psalms, the New Testament, and the gospels. As it turns out, listening is not a passive experience. Comprehending the ancient scriptures requires active listening. Faithfully interpreting the ancient scriptures is hard work.

We must listen carefully to consider how aspects of the ancient context compare with our current world. Sometimes the wisdom and truth of scriptures can be heard plainly across thousands of years. Examples include timeless commands like "Do not murder. Do not lie. Care for widows and orphans. Love your neighbor as yourself."

The Lessons

The people sit. One or two Lessons, as appointed, are read, the Reader first saying

A Reading (Lesson) from _____ .

A citation giving chapter and verse may be added.

After each Reading, the Reader may say

> The Word of the Lord.
People Thanks be to God.

or the Reader may say Here ends the Reading (Epistle).

Silence may follow.

A Psalm, hymn, or anthem may follow each Reading.

Then, all standing, the Deacon or a Priest reads the Gospel, first saying

> The Holy Gospel of our Lord Jesus Christ according to _____ .
People Glory to you, Lord Christ.

After the Gospel, the Reader says

> The Gospel of the Lord.
People Praise to you, Lord Christ.

—The service for Holy Communion continues on page 357 of *The Book of Common Prayer.*

We must also listen carefully to consider other parts of ancient context, which we must reject because they are no longer laudable or true. This includes mentions in scripture about the legality of slavery or capital punishment for all sorts of nonviolent misdemeanors.

Listening up means listening "between the lines" for the deepest meaning of a faithful life with God. Listening up means leaning in to hear the call of God, which still rings true and relevant across the ages, even when it reveals discrepancies with the ancient world in which the biblical narrative unfolded.

Both Saint Peter and Saint Paul hear something radically new and different from the law spelled out in their ancient scriptures of the Old Testament. Saint Peter listens "between the lines" and hears that nothing created by God is unclean. Saint Paul listens "between the lines" after he encounters Christ, and his conviction in the risen Lord leads him to confidently declare that *all* are one in Christ Jesus, Jew or Gentile, slave or owner, woman or man.

According to Saint Paul in his letter to the Romans, faith comes by hearing...by listening. Yet it is hard to listen well, isn't it? We would much rather see the answers written out before us in black and white. We would like to see with certainty all that we want and need to know—without ambiguity.

It is no coincidence that even in the beginning of creation, the man and woman did not see God in the garden. They could see the fruit—that magical shortcut to perfect knowledge, wisdom, and divinity itself. However, they could not see God; they could only listen.

Not surprisingly, the very first commandment, even before the Ten Commandments, is *Shema, Israel...*Hear, O Israel...Listen up, Israel! This is our commandment, too. Listening is what we are still called to do as an indispensable part of faithful living. In the service of Holy Eucharist, listening well and listening up are indispensable aspects of worship because faith comes by hearing. Finding our story with God requires careful listening.

One of the ways that the service of Holy Eucharist encourages careful listening is by offering us a sampling of readings from the Old Testament and the New Testament. These writings have been studied in minute detail for thousands of years, more than any other collection of writings in history.

Fortunately for us, many wise and faithful teachers have carefully curated these lessons so we can conveniently listen to how the words and deeds of Jesus compare with the stories of his ancestors, the exhortations of the prophets, the music of the psalmist, and the interpretation of all these things by letter-writers like Paul, Peter, James, and John.

When you listen carefully to the lessons in a service of Holy Eucharist, it is as if the story of God is being carefully expressed in a four or five-part harmony, drawing upon different voices from different places and times spanning thousands of miles and thousands of years. Sometimes they sound in unison. Sometimes there is dissonance. Oftentimes, there is a beautiful harmony expressing the peace, love, and joy of God, inviting the human family to listen up and sing along in our own words and deeds!

In fact, during the service of Holy Eucharist, a couple of subtle expressions of these words and deeds start us on our way. When we hear the lectors (readers) conclude the readings by saying, "The Word of the Lord," we respond with gratitude for being invited into this love story by saying, "Thanks be to God." We celebrate the Gospel of Jesus Christ as the core of this love story by holding the gospel book high and parading it into the midst of the people as Jesus, himself, entered the divine love story right in the midst of the people. And we salute this good news by announcing the gospel before *and* after the reading. All of us get to say, "Glory to you, Lord Christ" and also "Praise to you, Lord Christ." In both cases, we are recognizing that Jesus Christ is the Word of God, the clearest and most powerful expression of God's love in the world.

So, how do you hear God? What does it sound like when the Lord God walks through the garden at the time of the evening breeze? Is the sound of God a whisper in the wind or a mighty rumble of thunder and lightning?

Do you sometimes feel like the prophet Elijah, searching for God in the drama of earthquake, wind, and fire, only to find the divine voice in the sound of silence?[i]

Let's face it. If we had been in the garden and we were offered a choice between fruit we could immediately see, touch, and taste, along with a promise of enlightenment, or on the other hand, to wait around and listen to the plants grow, which option would we choose?

We still crave instant gratification today. We cling to the notion of a shortcut. The story of Genesis was not written as an historical account, but it is nonetheless true. We experience this truth as we relate to it thousands of years later. We still experience the temptations of greed, impatience, pride, and self-deification revealed in the garden in the beginning.

The 150 psalms of the Old Testament offer a comprehensive, prayerful, and musical reflection about God and what life with God is like. Exploring themes that harken all the way back to creation, these writings express some of the deepest, most visceral expressions of human longing to be found in all the scriptures.

Psalm 130 is also about listening but from a different perspective. The psalmist cries out to the Lord. From the depths of his soul, he cries out and begs God to hear him...to listen to him...to LISTEN UP!

Out of the depths have I called to you, O Lord;
Lord, hear my voice;
> let your ears consider well the voice of my
> > supplication.

If you, Lord, were to note what is done amiss,
> O Lord, who could stand?

For there is forgiveness with you;
> therefore you shall be feared.

I wait for the Lord, my soul waits for him;
> in his word is my hope.

My soul waits for the Lord,
more than watchmen for the morning,
> more than watchmen for the morning.

O Israel, wait for the Lord,
> for with the Lord there is mercy;

With him there is plenteous redemption,
> and he shall redeem Israel from all their sins.

—Psalm 130

Do you notice how the tables turn? Those of us who are visual learners, who seek shortcuts and are too busy to be still and pray, now beseech God to sit still and listen to us! And this God who walks in the garden at the time of the evening breeze calls back, just as in the story of Genesis, and asks, "Where *are* you? Where are *you*?"

At least the faithful psalmist was willing to meet God halfway. He was willing to wait for the Lord. "My soul waits for the Lord," he sang, "more than watchmen for the morning…more than watchmen for the morning."

†

My dad joined the army during World War II with the hope of learning to fly airplanes. He received an immediate promise that he would learn to fly. This promise did not come from God; it came from the recruiter who enlisted my father. Not all promises are created equal.

After my father finished boot camp, the officer in charge of deployment offered him three choices: mechanic school, mechanic school, mechanic school. Not surprisingly, my father chose mechanic school and learned how to help other soldiers fly safely across North Africa, up through Italy, and into Germany.

Part of my dad's job included taking turns as a watchman in the night, standing guard among the airplanes. Being a night watchman required vigilant listening, keen awareness, and a willing preparedness to respond to the unpredictable. Being present to God is not all that different—it requires vigilance in our listening, awareness and attention, and a willing preparedness to respond to the unpredictable.

Put simply, prayer is work. Perhaps that is why the Latin root of the word liturgy—*leitourgia*—expresses the centrality of *work* as part of the idea of worship.

How do you work at listening for God? How do you remain vigilant in your listening? What helps you stay aware and attentive? How do you stay prepared for our unpredictable God?

One night in North Africa, my father thought he heard something as he sat nestled into the base of a wing on one of the aircrafts. He drew his weapon and called out, "Halt! Who goes there?" No answer.

His eyes could not focus on any misplaced shape or movement as he scanned the darkened airfield. He called out again, "Halt! Who goes there?" A human shape suddenly emerged on the other side of the plane.

His commanding officer nearly lost his life by sneaking up on the watchman that evening because of reports that soldiers were crawling into cockpits and sleeping through their watch. My father was vigilant and attentive—and fortunately, prepared for the unpredictable act of arresting one's commanding officer instead of killing him.

The story of Genesis reminds us that there are no easy shortcuts. There are no surefire ways to know the fullness of truth without relying upon the mercy of God, which we seek in our prayer. There is no salvation without the "plenteous redemption"[ii] that God intends for all creation and for which we give thanks in our prayer.

So we must listen for the Lord God, without shame or fear, because our God longs to save us. We must wait for the Lord, more than watchmen for the morning, and trust that God will bring us out of the darkness and into the morning light.

"Shema! Hear, O Israel! Listen up, dear people of God!"

As Saint Paul taught the Corinthians, so he teaches us: "We look not at what can be seen, but at what cannot be seen...for what cannot be seen is eternal."[iii]

And since we cannot see our Lord God, we must listen. We must listen to what the scriptures tell us about God and what life with God is like. We must listen "between the lines" with vigilance because what is good and laudable and true in our world will not always resemble word for word what was considered good, laudable, and true in the ancient world.

We must be attentive and aware of our own stories of God's mercies and be prepared for God's unpredictable and miraculous ways.

Reflecting on Our Story with God

❖ Name a few times when you wanted quick and simple answers to difficult questions, but you waited patiently and listened more deeply to God's calling.

❖ Reflect on occasions when you saw obvious and convenient shortcuts but chose to read more carefully between the lines for a more subtle and truer truth.

❖ Why do you think God chooses to speak in silence to Elijah? How does God speak in silence to you?

Celebrating Our Story with God

❖ Give thanks for the careful listeners in your life who pay attention to stories of your joys and sorrows, hopes and concerns. Practice being a more careful listener of others.

❖ Memorize at least a portion of Psalm 130 as your own personal prayer for patience.

❖ Listen more attentively to the lessons you hear in worship as a means by which you come to understand your own story with God more clearly.

Chapter 6

The Sermon

Time to Dive In

Everyone will know that you are my disciples if you have love for one another.
—John 13:35

After various instructions and options pertaining to the reading of the lessons, the order of service for the Holy Eucharist in *The Book of Common Prayer* specifies one thing:

The Sermon

There are no further instructions. There are no other options. After lessons are read and the gospel proclaimed, the sermon is to be preached. I will never forget something my church history professor said in seminary, in part because I did not believe him at first. Dr. Don Armentrout stood before us and laid down the burden and challenge this way: "Work hard on your sermon. It is the most pastoral thing you will do all week."

After years of pastoring and preaching, I am now convinced he was right. At no other time during the week are so many people listening so carefully for an assurance that faith, hope, and love are alive—not just back when Jesus preached and fed and healed the people but also now when those of us who are living members of his Body are doing the preaching and feeding and healing in his name.

Across that span of two-thousand years, some things are very different, and some things are exactly the same. The work of a preacher is to help sort those things out for the congregation so that the faith, hope, and love of God is just as palpable now as it was then.

It is not accurate to say that the preacher needs to bring the Word to life, because the Word is already alive and well without the preacher. Still, the sermon is a special opportunity for someone to share not just a report of the Good News but an *experience* of the Good News.

Preachers who grasp this distinction are like careful translators in the ongoing conversation between God and the Church. The best sermons draw threads from the witness of scripture as well as the experience of the congregation and then weave them together. Preachers who do this are able to speak pastoral as well as challenging words, borne of a deep love for Christ and for the people who are the members of Christ's Body in the world today.

Preaching is to the gospel what celebrating is to the Holy Eucharist. Both of these gifts are enacted by the gathered community with the assistance of the preacher and the celebrant. Therefore, it is incumbent upon the preacher and celebrant to lead with enough preparation and conviction for the congregation to recognize their active role—not just *hearing out* what God is saying but *living out* what God is doing.

Søren Kierkegaard, the great Christian existentialist philosopher of the nineteenth century, described the experience of interacting with someone proficient in the details of biblical scholarship but who nonetheless failed to think deeply about the message: "It is almost like reading a cookbook when one is hungry."

Preachers must be mindful that people do not come to the Holy Eucharist in order to read or hear about what being fed might be like. They come purely and simply to be fed and therefore nourished and strengthened to be healthy, living members of Christ's Body. Every time I begin to prepare a sermon, I remind myself of a claim I once heard: On any given Sunday, about half the people in the congregation almost didn't come. If people who come to worship have an experience of the truth of how God's faith, hope, and love are alive in the world today, they are more likely to return and be fed and nourished again and again.

Water, bread, wine, and story are the Church's tangible gifts. When we use these gifts well, they communicate the kind of transformation spoken through the ancient prophets and fleshed out with a unique clarity by Jesus. The sermon— situated perfectly between the congregation hearing the lessons and speaking the creed—can serve as a gift that invites people to dive in to the mystery of experiencing life immersed in the faith, hope, and love of God.

Perhaps the best way to think of the sermon is to imagine it as an invitation to live with justice, peace, and fruitfulness in our relationships—with God, self, neighbor, and creation. After all, these virtues and relationships are the essence of righteousness as described in both the Old and New Testaments. Preachers and congregations who mindfully weave the threads of scripture and the experiences of our lives will always be discovering and sharing the stories that invite others more deeply into this kind of godly life.

In our Baptismal Covenant, we promise to "proclaim by word and example the Good News of God in Christ" (p. 305). This makes us all preachers, because to preach is to proclaim.

At the Last Supper as described in the Gospel according to John, Jesus demonstrates for his disciples a way to be effective preachers. After using water, bread, and wine to communicate about transformation, Jesus returns to their story—their lived experience together—in order to show them how to preach by word and example. In one new commandment, Jesus tells all of us disciples how to invite others to experience life immersed in the faith, hope, and love of God.

> I give you a new commandment, that you love one another. Just as I have loved you, you also should love one another. By this everyone will know that you are my disciples, if you have love for one another."
>
> —John 13:34-35

†

The smell of chlorine was overpowering, but that was not all. The screaming noise of a swim meet rattles even the strongest nerves. At the Jewish Community Center in Columbia, South

Carolina, the starting gun crackled loudly, and all the young Jewish swimmers took off.

On the ledge of that pool stood a solitary Gentile with her knees locked in fear. She was five years old, and it was her very first swim meet. She had learned how to stay afloat only two weeks earlier. Everything was brand new, and she was terrified. Finley Buchanan was the Gentile, the outsider. She was literally the one outside the pool although she belonged as much as anyone else.

The Jewish parents paused from cheering their own children, and they began cheering for the frightened, five-year-old Gentile. God bless those adults and their encouragement for my child who stood there, trembling, shaking, and wringing her hands. Still, the cheering in the distance was not enough to get her into the pool where she belonged.

On the opposite end of the pool was another child standing on the concrete ledge. "Jump in, Finley!" shouted her older sister. "Swim to me! You can do it!" Katherine's eight-year-old voice, loud as it was, simply wasn't enough. She waved her arms, trying to beckon her little sister to dive in to the water. Nothing happened. Sometimes you have to do more than cheer in the distance.

God bless all the children in our lives who are unafraid to show us—by words and examples—new ways to live and new ways to love. Katherine was positively determined Finley would swim her first race, and so Katherine—in absolute and total violation of the rules—dove into the pool and swam in the opposite direction of all the other competing swimmers. She raced to within a few feet of Finley; as she treaded water, she looked up and said, "Come on, Finley, I'll swim *with* you." Guess who dove into the pool where she belonged!

Sometimes you have to break the rules to do the right thing. Sometimes you have to go in the opposite direction of everyone else to do a new thing. Sometimes, fulfilling Christ's new commandment to love one another requires more than cheering in the distance.

The best song of 1989, according to the Oscars, the Grammys, and the Golden Globe Awards, is Carly Simon's hymn to New York entitled "Let the River Run." She wrote the song for a movie, not as a political or religious statement. Still, inspired by the poetry of Walt Whitman and perhaps William Blake, she penned these words:

"Let the river run, let all the dreamers wake the nation. Come, the New Jerusalem! We're coming to the edge, running on the water, coming through the fog, your sons and daughters."

When I hear that song, I think of my daughters standing on the edge, hoping and dreaming, and then diving in and swimming in the water. Nothing that Katherine Buchanan accomplishes in her life will make me as proud as I already am of her love-inspired actions on that day. And I think this is how our heavenly Father sees us, too. Nothing we can ever accomplish in any material sense will ever mean as much as when we stop cheering in the distance and dive in to do whatever it takes to love one another as Christ loves us.

When I hear Carly Simon's song, I also imagine a Church filled with dreamers who help wake the nation with words and examples of the new commandment to "Love one another as I have loved you." I dream of a Church investing in Saint John's Revelation of a new heaven and a new earth, where the old, dominating patterns of the past are cast aside, the New Jerusalem comes down, and God dwells with us on earth as in heaven (Revelation 21:1-6).

In nineteenth-century England, William Blake articulated this message in his social justice poem, set to the music of the hymn *Jerusalem*. And Carl Daw, an Episcopal priest, reflected Isaiah's prophetic dream in the lyrics:

"O day of peace that dimly shines through all our hopes and prayers and dreams, guide us to justice, truth, and love, delivered from our selfish schemes. May swords of hate fall from our hands, our hearts from envy find release, till by God's grace our warring world shall see Christ's promised reign of peace.

Then shall the wolf dwell with the lamb, nor shall the fierce devour the small; as beasts and cattle calmly graze, a little child shall lead them all. Then enemies shall learn to love, all creatures find their true accord; the hope of peace shall be fulfilled, for all the earth shall know the Lord."[iv]

The sermon, proclaimed by beloved children of God by word and example, invites others to experience the faith, hope, and love of a God who has made all things new—new dreams, new songs, a new commandment, even a vision of a new heaven and a new earth. This is not the kind of bland news about which one can simply cheer from a distance. It is Good News that defies our expectations and calls us to dive right in for the sake of love.

As you listen to the words of the sermon during the Holy Eucharist, consider how that proclamation informs and inspires your own call to proclaim the Good News by word and example out in the world. Even though the Holy Eucharist specifies one sermon during worship, the truth is that the experience of the Good News throughout the service should propagate many sermons that we live out in our daily lives.

Saint Francis said, "It is no use walking anywhere to preach unless our walking is our preaching." This lovely quotation is a reminder to walk in love as Christ loves us, an echo of Jesus' words proclaimed at the Last Supper: "Everyone will know you are my disciples if you have love for one another."

Reflecting on Our Story with God

❖ Try to remember a sermon that made a particularly strong impression on you. What had a particularly transforming or inspiring effect?

❖ Now try to remember when someone (not standing in a pulpit) proclaimed by word or example the Good News of God in Christ. What had a particularly transforming or inspiring effect?

Celebrating Our Story with God

❖ In 500 words or less, write an account of an experience you have had of faith, hope, or love that helped you trust enough to "dive in" to where you belong. Identify a close friend or family member with whom you feel comfortable sharing this story, and pass it along.

❖ Think of one or two actions that you could perform with deeds rather than with words that would proclaim the Good News as Jesus proposed—by loving one another as he loves us. If these examples defy expectations, all the better! Now go out and "preach" these sermons without necessarily saying a word.

Chapter 7

The Nicene Creed

Clear for Takeoff

Jesus said, "Do not let your hearts be troubled. Believe in God, believe also in me."

—John 14:1

Affirming our story with God is the work of the people. The preacher, choir, and other leaders read, sing, and interpret God's story, but the people gathered are charged with affirming this story as our own.

At celebrations of Holy Baptism, we use the Apostles' Creed. Although similar to the Nicene Creed, the subject pronoun in the Apostles' Creed is "I." The person being baptized, the parents and godparents, and the entire community affirm their individual response to God's grace: "I believe in God, the Father….I believe in Jesus Christ…I believe in the Holy Spirit."[v]

However, at all other celebrations of the Holy Eucharist the words we use to affirm our faith come from the Nicene Creed. The subject pronoun in the Nicene Creed is "We." *We believe* is a first-person-plural enterprise.

The Nicene Creed

We believe in one God,
    the Father, the Almighty,
    maker of heaven and earth,
    of all that is, seen and unseen.

We believe in one Lord, Jesus Christ,
    the only Son of God,
    eternally begotten of the Father,
    God from God, Light from Light,
    true God from true God,
    begotten, not made,
    of one Being with the Father.
    Through him all things were made.
    For us and for our salvation
        he came down from heaven:
    by the power of the Holy Spirit
        he became incarnate from the Virgin Mary,
        and was made man.
    For our sake he was crucified under Pontius Pilate;
        he suffered death and was buried.
        On the third day he rose again
            in accordance with the Scriptures;
        he ascended into heaven
            and is seated at the right hand of the Father.
    He will come again in glory to judge the living
                    and the dead,
        and his kingdom will have no end.

We believe in the Holy Spirit, the Lord, the giver of life,
    who proceeds from the Father and the Son.

With the Father and the Son he is worshiped and glorified.
He has spoken through the Prophets.
We believe in one holy catholic and apostolic Church.
We acknowledge one baptism for the forgiveness of sins.
We look for the resurrection of the dead,
    And the life of the world to come. Amen.

—The service for Holy Communion continues
on page 358 of *The Book of Common Prayer*.

Using the Nicene Creed as a central component in our service
of Holy Eucharist signals that faith is a shared experience in
which we all have an affirming part. Celebrating our story
with God is not a self-promoting, end-zone dance but rather
a team sport with bumps and bruises, wins and losses that are
part of living in community.

Some people are put off by religion because they equate
"being religious" with a ridiculous emphasis on a lengthy set
of beliefs. This sour taste becomes even more acute when the
conspicuous actions (or inactions) of the "believers" do not
match what they say.

Many skeptics—including me—have a hard time not reacting
cynically to the wide, yawning gap between those who say one
thing and do another. We hear the relentless litany of beliefs to
which one is expected to give lip service, and we decide there
must be more to life than pretending to sign on for all of that.

I suggest another way of looking at the creeds. Instead of
seeing the creeds primarily as guides to what we have to think,
let's examine them through the lens of how they help us to

practice our faith. We have a pretty good example for this approach in Jesus, who seemed to care very little about what people thought of him—positively or negatively. He cared far more about how people practiced faith that produced healing, freedom, justice, and peace.

The word creed comes from the Latin *credo*, the etymology of which relates to matters of the heart. So when we affirm our faith in the words of a creed, we are really affirming what (or who) is deserving of our heart. A good, challenging exercise for skeptics as well as believers is to write one's own creed. To what or to whom are you willing to give your heart? To what—or to whom—are you wholehearted?

I affirm my faith in the words of the historic creeds because they best express in simple language the basic but profound truths I have come to hold about the creative, redeeming, sustaining love of God. They are not so much a litmus test of what I need to think but rather an illumination of how I want to have faith and life in concert with this miraculous love of God.

When I join my voice with others and say, "We believe," I am expressing something simple and basic about the One to whom we are willing to give our heart and soul with hope that this faith will help us to bring about healing, freedom, justice, and peace in God's name.

I am not saying this is easy. Sometimes it is hard to know what to believe—as Jesus' own disciples demonstrated. This is part of the reason it helps that the subject pronoun in our regular creed is "We." Jesus, after all, called not just one disciple but twelve.

Although the Nicene Creed has a bit about the Father and the Holy Spirit, it is mostly about Jesus. Saint Paul taught the Colossians that "Jesus is the image of the invisible God"—the One we can see, hear, and touch. As such, Jesus is the one who points us to—and through—things we do not understand. Jesus is the one who helps us have faith when we don't know what to believe.

Yet, with the disciples (and that means us, too), it sometimes feels like Jesus thinks too highly of our capacity to understand and be faithful. This brings us back to the creed—a gift to help us affirm not what we know or even what we think we know but simply to affirm the One to whom we give our *credo*, our hearts.

Affirming our story with God is all about affirming our desire to journey with Christ, in spite of our disbeliefs, doubts, and fears. One of the best stories from the Bible that illustrates this doubt and desire is the story about Saint Thomas talking with Jesus after the Last Supper. Saint Thomas—of doubting fame— knew what it felt like to struggle with beliefs and skepticism, with hopes and fears.

> Jesus said, "Do not let your hearts be troubled. Believe in God, believe also in me. In my Father's house there are many dwelling-places. If it were not so, would I have told you that I go to prepare a place for you? And if I go and prepare a place for you, I will come again and will take you to myself, so that where I am, there you may be also. And you know the way to the place where I am going."
>
> Thomas said to him, "Lord, we do not know where you are going. How can we know the way?" Jesus said to him, "I am the way, and the truth, and the life. No one comes to the Father except through me. If you know

me, you will know my Father also. From now on you do know him and have seen him."

Philip said to him, "Lord, show us the Father, and we will be satisfied." Jesus said to him, "Have I been with you all this time, Philip, and you still do not know me? Whoever has seen me has seen the Father. How can you say, 'Show us the Father?' Do you not believe that I am in the Father and the Father is in me? The words that I say to you I do not speak on my own; but the Father who dwells in me does his works. Believe me that I am in the Father and the Father is in me; but if you do not, then believe me because of the works themselves. Very truly, I tell you, the one who believes in me will also do the works that I do and, in fact, will do greater works than these, because I am going to the Father. I will do whatever you ask in my name, so that the Father may be glorified in the Son. If in my name you ask me for anything, I will do it."

—John 14:1-14

In the Gospel according to Saint John, Jesus spends the night following the Last Supper addressing the anxieties of his disciples. They want to follow him, but they are confused and afraid. Jesus urges them not to let their hearts be troubled, but they remain anxious about what to do and where to turn. Thomas says, "Lord, we do not know where you are going. How can we know the way?"

This is where I think Thomas gets a bad rap. His question should not dub him "Doubting Thomas." Rather, his question comes from an absolutely overwhelmed Thomas. It is not that he lacks faith in Jesus; he simply lacks confidence in himself. Thomas does not know what to do or how to think or where to turn. It is easy for us to relate to Thomas—we

want so badly to believe and yet we do not always know
what to think.

Likewise, the disciple Philip says, "Lord, show us the Father,
and we will be satisfied." Philip is not being carelessly skeptical
nor does he lack commitment. He simply lacks clarity. We can
also relate to Philip—we want so badly to trust and yet we do
not always see enough to feel confident in that trust.

†

When I was about eight years old, I remember being absolutely
overwhelmed, like Thomas. Everything around me was buzzing
so loudly that I could barely hear anything at all. The sun
was uncomfortably warm. All I could see was a narrow slice
of blue sky above and dozens of cryptic numbers and gauges
shimmering and rattling right before my eyes.

I was sitting as tall as possible, buckled into the co-pilot's seat
of a Cessna single-engine airplane. There was an alarming
crackle, and then a nearly indiscernible voice that spoke only
three words: "Clear for takeoff."

It was not that I lacked faith in my father; I simply lacked
confidence in myself. It was not that I lacked commitment;
I simply lacked clarity. I wanted so badly to trust, and yet I
could not see enough to feel sure.

The terrifying and thrilling acceleration is something you never
forget—not just on an airport runway but also crossing a stage
at graduation or starting a new job, beginning a marriage or
moving to a new place or entering a different phase of life. It is
terrifying and thrilling at the same time. And so Jesus still tells
his disciples, "Do not let your hearts be troubled. Believe in
God, believe also in me."

When we lack confidence in ourselves, we must cultivate our trust in those who have gone before us. This is one of the gifts of the church—offering us the witness of saints.

In that airplane, I could neither reach the floor pedals nor see the center line on the asphalt, so my father steered the plane down the middle of the runway. As we gained speed, the warm summer air began to flirt with the wings, although the tires still bumped and skipped along. If I had known where the brakes were, I would have hit them.

If Thomas and Philip had known how to hit the brakes, I think they would have! They were overwhelmed, and they lacked confidence—not in Jesus, but in themselves. Why wouldn't they be overwhelmed in the midst of uncertainty? Why wouldn't they lack confidence when they had not faced such a terrifying and thrilling acceleration toward a heavenly transition?

Why shouldn't we be overwhelmed in our uncertainty? Why shouldn't we lack confidence not having practiced all the faith that is promised to us?

This points to yet another gift of the church: companions who travel with us on this journey, which is filled with promise and yet still requires practice and experience. We want to be spiritual—floating contentedly from cloud to cloud—but we still need help getting off the ground and coping with the clouds that turn into storms.

Just when I thought I could not take it anymore, my dad gently pulled back on his steering handle. My white-knuckled fingers, clasped around the co-pilot's handle, could feel the smooth movement because the two steering columns were yoked together as one. The tires hushed their frantic turning and the mystery of climbing into thin air opened right before my very eyes. I cut a glance to the left, and I could see my father smiling, just like he did every single time in the face of this mystery.

When we celebrate the service of Holy Eucharist, we are smiling in the face of mysteries we cannot fully understand or control. We are challenged to look beyond the closest horizons of our lives with the assurance that we do not travel alone. Jesus still tells his disciples, "Do not let your hearts be troubled. Believe in God, believe also in me."

How can we believe when we cannot see? Seeing is believing, isn't it? We would like to see the questions on the test. We would like to know the answers to our problems. We would like to have the secrets to success. We crave certainty—we desire it with white-knuckled fingers, clasped tightly onto whatever handles give us a grip. Often, the things we grip do not lift us up, after all.

When I was overwhelmed and ready to hit the brakes, I found the peace that is found when we realize we are yoked with One who knows the way, who will love us through our fears and lift us up.

This is the essence of life between the Father and the Son— the very thing Jesus is trying to explain to Philip. Jesus says, "Believe me that I am in the Father and the Father is in me..." In other words, they are perfectly yoked to one another, "God from God, Light from Light, true God from true God."[vi]

On this earthly journey we look to Jesus, the pioneer and perfecter of our faith, who not only knows the way but who is The Way. He has prepared the way for us, knowing full well that we are overwhelmed at times, that we sometimes lack confidence, that we cannot see beyond our closest horizons.

And so he still tells us disciples, "Do not let your hearts be troubled. Believe in God, believe also in me."

The good (and alarming) news in this gospel story about confusion and fear is that we are clear for take-off, regardless of whether we feel ready. The other good news from this story is that we are not alone. We simply have to hold on in faith as we discover the peace and promise of being yoked to the loving Christ who is the way, the truth, and the life that we need.

He will lift us up to become all that we have been created to be—people whose *credo* makes it possible for us to have faith, look beyond our closest horizons, and smile in the face of such wonderful mystery.

When we affirm our story with God in the words of the Nicene Creed, we are trying to reach beyond certainty and get a grip alongside the One we have met—Jesus, the image of the invisible God. We are holding on for the ride, trusting that he is perfectly yoked with God our Father and with us. And we are praying that this miraculous Love will bring about faith and life that produces healing, freedom, justice, and peace on earth as it is in heaven.

Reflecting on Our Story with God

❖ Try to remember a time you were overwhelmed with doubt or fear and held onto someone you trusted.

❖ Reflect on an occasion when you were lifted up by someone or something other than your own strength. What was it like to smile in the face of this mystery? What was it like to look beyond your own horizon?

Celebrating Our Story with God

❖ Write a personal creed about the beliefs, priorities, or virtues about which you are wholehearted. How does your statement compare, contrast, amplify, or diminish how you affirm your trust in the power of love?

❖ Now write a collective creed about what you and your neighbors—fellow parishioners or fellow citizens—could agree upon in terms of beliefs, priorities, and virtues. In what ways could it be more expansive? More limiting?

❖ Consider the practical differences between certainty and faith, between knowledge and trust. Where is God calling you? In what areas are you struggling between these concepts?

Chapter 8

The Prayers of the People

Jesus, Jesus, Jesus

Then everyone who calls upon the name of the Lord will be saved.

—Acts 2:21

After we affirm our *credo*—our hearty response to the love of God—then we practice fleshing out that response by offering the deepest, most sincere expressions we carry within our hearts. We express our joy and gratitude, our lament and regret, our pain and fear. We have the chance to offer all these things, either silently or aloud, during the prayers of the people.

First of all, notice that the liturgy clearly describes these as the prayers of the people, not the prayers of the priest. In other words, prayer is not reserved for spiritual experts and holy specialists. Prayer belongs to all people, as surely as the full, sincere truths of deep joy, sadness, regret, hope, and fear reside in the human hearts of all people.

The Prayers of the People

Prayer is offered with intercession for

The Universal Church, its members, and its mission
The Nation and all in authority
The welfare of the world
The concerns of the local community
Those who suffer and those in any trouble
The departed (with commemoration of a saint when appropriate)

—The service for Holy Communion continues on page 359 of *The Book of Common Prayer*.

Ideally, someone from within the congregation steps forward to lead these prayers of the people. *The Book of Common Prayer* offers six different "ready-made forms" for these prayers, though the clergy and people of congregations often write their own prayers of thanksgiving and intercession to use in these moments.

The exact form or substance is not dictated, so long as the time of prayer is inclusive of the range of people, places, and things that faithful communities should hold in their prayerful attention. We should, of course, remember the members and mission of the Universal Church, that wonderful and sacred mystery, and not just our own little part of it. Praying for the whole Church restores our awareness of the fullness of Christ's Body in the world.

We also remember our nation in prayer as well as all those in authority (whether we like them or not). We pray for our nation and its leaders because of the difference they—and we—can collectively make for justice and peace.

We pray for the welfare of the world, even though we don't have the slightest chance of making much impact upon the entire world's welfare—by ourselves. But when we join collectively in prayers for the world, throughout the world, who knows what God will do! It is important for us to overcome the temptation of nationalistic thinking about God's blessings and recall the truth of John 3:16 that "God so loved the world that he gave his only Son."

We also pray closer to home, for the needs of our local communities. These are the places where our prayers in thought and word can lead us to prayers in deed as we strive for justice and peace in our own neighborhoods, parishes, and cities.

We always pray for those who suffer or find themselves in any need or trouble. If we ourselves are suffering, it is comforting to hear that we are remembered. If we are content, this prayer keeps us mindful of more than ourselves and our temporary privilege.

Finally, we remember those who have died. For some people, this seems strange unless we remember that in God's eyes, their life has changed, not ended. We also pray for the dead not because they need it but because it is an act of love we continue to offer, like putting flowers on a grave. After all, love is the thing that unites us all to God in Christ, both the living and the dead.

As we pray through these different intercessions, the leader of the prayers of the people should allow enough silence for all the gathered people to recount, recite, mumble, cry, or sigh through their recollection of people, places, and things that they carry deep within their hearts.

In Saint Paul's Letter to the Romans, he admits that "we do not know how to pray as we ought, but that very Spirit" of God helps us in our weakness, interceding "with sighs too deep for words" (8:26). During the prayers of the people, the words spoken by the intercessor (the one leading the prayers) help guide us. Yet, there are no "magic words" that prompt God to act as we want in a particular situation.

Sometimes the sincerest prayer of all is the silent sigh that Saint Paul describes as "too deep for words." Some of the most meaningful prayers I have offered for people are silent tears of solidarity, standing beside someone who is grieving while resisting the temptation to cheapen the moment by filling the air with anxious words. After all, the first language of the heart is love, and sometimes we practice its vocabulary best in the silence of truth that cannot be contained or expressed in words.

On the other hand, sometimes we want or need to speak our prayers out loud. There is a wonderful freedom during the prayers of the people to simply name the people for whom we pray—without guise of fancy vocabulary or elegant prose. God knows our needs before we ask, but if it helps you to speak aloud as a means of actualizing your prayer, this is your moment to join the chorus of others who do so as well.

Jesus gives some liberating counsel about praying, especially for those of us who feel like we never find the right words when called upon to pray. Jesus' teaching encourages us to simply offer our prayers sincerely.

Whenever you pray, do not be like the hypocrites; for
they love to stand and pray in the synagogues and at the
street corners, so that they may be seen by others. Truly I
tell you, they have received their reward...When you are
praying, do not heap up empty phrases as the Gentiles
do; for they think that they will be heard because of their
many words. Do not be like them, for your Father knows
what you need before you ask him.

—Matthew 6:5, 7

†

I was once in a frightening situation that called for prayer,
and I found myself caught off guard by the chorus of people
praying all around me. A few weeks into my solo journey
around the world, I landed in Ghana, West Africa. The people
of Ghana are among the most gentle and tender people I have
ever met. Yet, civil order and gentleness broke down in one
venue—the bus station in Accra.

Transportation was so scarce that throngs of people lunged
for the door of every empty bus that arrived in the hot, dusty
terminal. After several unsuccessful attempts of trying to elbow
my way onto a bus bound for the city of Kumasi, a couple of
strangers took pity on the disheveled teenager.

They offered to lift me up when the next bus pulled up to
the boarding area so I could climb through one of the little
windows near the back. The next bus arrived, and the three of
us ran for it. I took off my backpack, and they shoved me head
first through the back window.

After I righted myself, I watched in disbelief as adults, children,
the elderly, babies—and an occasional chicken—crammed

onto the bus, sitting, standing, crouching, and filling every conceivable space. Some passengers who could not fit inside scampered atop onto the luggage rack or clung to the sides of the front hood and side view mirrors. It was hot, and we were mashed and wedged together. It was as if we were one body.

The bus struggled to move with such a payload, but eventually we got to the main highway, by which time the exterior passengers had jumped off. The bus finally picked up speed. Somehow, my exhaustion and the hum of the engine caused me to doze off lightly as I sat in the back row, propped up by the mass of people jammed around me.

Suddenly I was shocked awake, startled by a violent, screaming noise that turned out to be an exploding and unraveling tire and the friction of a bare, front wheel against gravel. Then, there was more screaming inside the bus, "JESUS, JESUS, JESUS."

Like an angry bull, the bus lurched off the highway and raced down an embankment, "JESUS, JESUS, JESUS," smashing through a concrete wall, "JESUS, JESUS, JESUS," and mowing its way through a grove of banana trees. We finally came to a stop. The bus remained upright, and incredibly, there were only bruises, cuts, and scrapes.

Where I grew up, shouting "JESUS, JESUS, JESUS" in a loud voice was as bad as saying a curse word. It was a swearing of the worst sort, literally taking the Lord's name in vain. What I learned that day is that the people on the crowded bus were not swearing at all. They were calling out to someone they knew and trusted. They were well acquainted with their utter dependence upon God.

They weren't making a social call on a distant friend. They were making a desperate call on someone as near as the person wedged against them, on a person with a reputation for compassion. In other words, they called out to the One who suffers with us in our trials.

Jesus says, "Not everyone who says to me, 'Lord, Lord' will enter the kingdom of heaven. To some I will declare that I never knew you" (Matthew 7:21, 23). So where do we find our hope?

We will not find it in our own power, no matter how powerful we are. Our hope is found in a relationship with a living God who meets us where we are in the midst of our deepest needs when we express the sincerest truth of our hearts—either silently or aloud—by calling upon the name of the Lord in prayer.

We will not find hope in our money, no matter how wealthy we are. Our hope is found in a relationship with a living God who meets us in places where money is worthless to make things better, places where we must ask for help like everyone else by calling upon the name of the Lord in prayer.

We will not find hope in our personal respectability, no matter how respectable we are. Our hope is found in a relationship with a living God who meets us on the highway, like the Good Samaritan—bringing healing and hope for stranded souls like us who recognize our utter dependence on God's mercy and call upon the name of the Lord in prayer.

When Jesus predicts that some people will hear him say "I never knew you," he is telling us that the kingdom of heaven is not about us. God's kingdom is not defined (or limited) by our power, wealth, or personal respectability. God's kingdom is all about relationship with a living God whose compassion and mercy are boundless for those who ask for it by calling upon the name of the Lord in prayer.

So where do we begin? We begin with our prayers to the Jesus we know and love. The prayers of the people are our opportunity to make a personal call upon the One who is near and compassionate. Moreover, we offer our prayers together because we find our hope through relationships—with God and one another.

Being in the church is a lot like being on that crowded bus headed for Kumasi. First of all, somebody helped us on the bus, and we should give thanks for that relationship and for their kindness in bringing us aboard.

Second, as crowded and uncomfortable as it can sometimes be, we should give thanks that we are shoved together like one body—because those relationships often help cushion the bumps and bruises that come our way.

And finally, when things are falling apart, we should give thanks that we can call on Jesus, whom we are getting to know more intimately, whose name we are learning to trust more deeply, and whose compassion we are growing to accept more recklessly.

It is all about relationships! It is about getting to know the One we call "Lord, Lord" so that he won't say, "I never knew you."

The Office of Morning Prayer includes a prayer for mission that very clearly conveys that Jesus' embrace is for *everyone*. It also reminds us to reach forth our hands in love as we embrace compassion through prayer in word and deed.

"Lord Jesus Christ, you stretched out your arms of love on the hard wood of the cross that everyone might come within the reach of your saving embrace: So clothe us in your Spirit that we, reaching forth our hands in love, may bring those who do not know you to the knowledge and love of you; for the honor of your Name" (*The Book of Common Prayer*, p. 101).

It is a gift to bring the knowledge and love of God to people who have not found their way onto the bus and to help them climb aboard. It is a gift to reach forth our hands in love to those who are in need of some compassion. It is a gift to share the saving embrace of Jesus with one another and to be the Body of Christ.

Most of all, it is a gift to call out to the One who knows us, loves us, and wants nothing more or less than to be in a compassionate relationship with us and all the wrecked, broken-down souls who call upon his name.

So, join in the prayers of the people—either silently or aloud—not worrying about "magic words" or elegant prose but expressing the first language of your heart, the language of love. These prayers give you the chance to express the sincere truths of the joy, sadness, regret, hope, and fear that reside in your heart, just as they do in the hearts of all people.

This is your moment to call upon the name of a Lord we can trust, the One with whom we find compassion. And his name is *Jesus, Jesus, Jesus.*

Reflecting on Our Story with God

❖ Remember the person(s) who helped you "get on board" the church and encounter the compassion of Jesus, and give thanks.

❖ Reflect on a time when a community of people helped cushion bumps or bruises you may have experienced in your life, and give thanks.

❖ Think of a time when things were falling apart, and you called upon the compassion of Jesus. Give thanks for a Lord who is not just high and lofty but also low and vulnerable as One who suffers with us.

Celebrating Our Story with God

❖ Make a mental or written list of the people, places, and things you would like to remember in your prayers. Offer your sincere expressions of love on behalf of these, silently and aloud, at home and when you keep the prayers of the people in worship.

❖ Consider writing prayers in your own words and collecting them in a journal you can keep near your bed or kitchen table or wherever you like to pray.

❖ Try rewriting some of your thanksgivings and intercessions in the form of personal notes to the people you keep in your prayers. Perhaps it could be helpful and encouraging for them to know that you are holding them in your prayers.

Chapter 9

Confession & Absolution

Leaving Baggage Behind

Therefore confess your sins to one another, and pray for one another, so that you may be healed. The prayer of the righteous is powerful and effective.

—James 5:16

The prayers of the people often conclude with a spoken confession. This is an opportunity for the gathered community to admit out loud: We are not perfect. Where else in the world do we have the opportunity to speak this truth? Where else in the world do we have the chance to be set free from this burden? I don't know of many other venues where this basic, honest assessment of daily life is articulated.

By acknowledging our faults—in thought, word, and deed— we can be restored to the kind of full and healthy relationship with God and neighbor that God desires and makes possible for us. However, God will not impose this gift upon us. We must acknowledge what we need and ask for forgiveness and reconciliation.

Confession of Sin

A Confession of Sin is said here if it has not been said earlier. On occasion, the Confession may be omitted.

One of the sentences from the Penitential Order on page 351 may be said.

The Deacon or Celebrant says

Let us confess our sins against God and our neighbor.

Silence may be kept.

Minister and People

Most merciful God,
we confess that we have sinned against you
in thought, word, and deed,
by what we have done,
and by what we have left undone.
We have not loved you with our whole heart;
we have not loved our neighbors as ourselves.
We are truly sorry and we humbly repent.
For the sake of your Son Jesus Christ,
have mercy on us and forgive us;
that we may delight in your will,
and walk in your ways,
to the glory of your Name. Amen.

The Bishop when present, or the Priest, stands and says

Almighty God have mercy on you, forgive you all your sins
through our Lord Jesus Christ, strengthen you in all
goodness, and by the power of the Holy Spirit keep you in
eternal life. *Amen.*

—The service for Holy Communion continues
on page 359 of *The Book of Common Prayer.*

I was on retreat at a monastery when I had a vivid experience of the importance of confessing something and receiving the blessing of being forgiven and restored. This is not a story about a confessional booth; it is a story about the way life happens and presents us with the need to acknowledge what we need but cannot give ourselves.

I was staying in a guest house near enough to the cloister to walk over to the chapel and yet far enough away not to disturb the cycle of the community's prayer and work. It was a cold night, and during the evening I built a roaring, hot fire in the fireplace.

At about 9 p.m. I stepped outside to get another log from the woodpile. I pulled the door behind me to keep the cold air out of the house, and it clicked shut...with the lock engaged! I had left the key on the kitchen counter, right next to my cell phone.

In the simplest terms, I had two choices. I could stand in the cold, shivering and looking at the blazing fire through the window (and praying that it would not emit sparks onto the carpet since I had pulled back the fire screen to add another log), or I could run over to the convent, confess what I had done, admit that I needed another key, and get back inside the cabin where I was supposed to be.

It was an easy, if embarrassing, choice to acknowledge my fault and receive what I needed. But even though this was an obvious choice, it's also a clear example of what forgiveness is. It is the peace of receiving a gift. It is the peace of having locked doors re-opened. Confession enables us to receive forgiveness and be restored to the fullness of the life we are intended to live.

Jesus has a lot to say about forgiveness of sins. He teaches us to pray for this forgiveness, even as we offer it to others who have trespassed against us. When Jesus teaches us to pray, "forgive us our sins *as we forgive those who sin against us,*" he reminds us not to ask or expect God to forgive us any more than we are willing to practice that same forgiveness.

Matthew's Gospel offers an important teaching about forgiveness. In the following passage, Jesus challenges us to say and do the things that acknowledge our faults and lead us to reconciliation. He tells us to admit what we need so we can be restored to fullness in our relationships. In other words, Jesus teaches an undeniable truth about leaving behind the heavy baggage.

> Jesus said, "If another member of the church sins against you, go and point out the fault when the two of you are alone. If the member listens to you, you have regained that one. But if you are not listened to, take one or two others along with you, so that every word may be confirmed by the evidence of two or three witnesses. If the member refuses to listen to them, tell it to the church; and if the offender refuses to listen even to the church, let such a one be to you as a Gentile and a tax-collector. Truly I tell you, whatever you bind on earth will be bound in heaven, and whatever you loose on earth will be loosed in heaven. Again, truly I tell you, if two of you agree on earth about anything you ask, it will be done for you by my Father in heaven. For where two or three are gathered in my name, I am there among them."
>
> —Matthew 18:15-20

✝

A good friend was traveling several years ago on a flight that terminated in Atlanta. He had been away on business for quite some time. The duration of this particular trip required him to use his very largest suitcase—an old, weary bag capable of hauling two weeks' worth of clothes, with room left to bring gifts and surprises for the family.

It is a pain hauling such a heavy bag from long-term parking, through the terminal to the ticketing counter, and then, upon returning home, to carry it from baggage claim back to the parking lot.

On this particular occasion, it turned out to be even more of a hassle. As the suitcases moved around the carousel, he watched in perfect horror as his giant, antique bag stuffed full of dirty clothes and gifts burst open at the base of the conveyor belt.

Olive oil, shirts, balsamic vinegar, underwear, toothpaste, socks, and a can of shaving cream decorated the carousel. The experience laid bare an undeniable truth: Carrying heavy baggage is no way to travel, if you can avoid it.

Saint Paul—quite a traveler himself—understands this intuitively. In his letters to the early churches, Paul advises the people to travel light, to let go of the heavy things that hold them (and us) back—baggage like anger, fear, pride, and prejudice. Paul exhorts the people to trust God to call all of us to a future that is even more than we can ask or imagine.[vii]

Often, we pride ourselves as people who travel light—we aren't carrying works of darkness, as described by Saint Paul to the Ephesians. We like to think of ourselves as totally—or at least mostly—innocent of the kinds of sins Paul describes. Others carry that heavy baggage around but not us.

But our lessons on packing come not only from Saint Paul but also from our Lord. Jesus tells us to examine the baggage we hold tightly because of other peoples' sins against us. Jesus is clear: He expects us to not only lay aside our sins but also to put aside other people's sins against us. Jesus expects us to not only let go of our shortcomings but also to relinquish other people's shortcomings that disappoint us.

What heavy baggage are you carrying? Are you having trouble letting go of certain angers and resentments?

Jesus personally knows that this tendency is all too human. We all pick up this kind of baggage from time to time and carry it around. And then, we often take the next step of wanting to share our baggage with others, perhaps hoping they will become incensed on our behalf. Just look at how often this takes place in the political discourse of our nation. The energy devoted to talking about ideas often devolves into maliciousness and slander about the people we want to blame.

It happens in the Church too. We stew and get angry about decisions or positions taken in our local congregations and in the wider Church, and we quickly become mired in resentment and bitterness for those we believe are to blame.

It can be unsettling to realize that Jesus rarely points the finger at sinners who are blameworthy but frequently criticizes those who are offended. For example, Jesus pardons the woman caught in adultery even as he shames all the men who appear to be so offended by her. Likewise, Jesus regularly eats and associates with notorious sinners while ridiculing those who pretend to be wiser and more holy.

In other words, Jesus devotes the bulk of his "heavy baggage" teaching to people like you and me. Jesus places the burden of forgiveness directly on the shoulders of the offended, not the offender. We may not always like this, but this is what Jesus asks of us.

The comforting thing about the confession during the Holy Eucharist is that we promise collectively to do what Jesus asks us to do. With our own voice alongside the voices of everyone else, we confess aloud our sorrow for all the things we have done and left undone.

This is sometimes referred to as the corporate confession—the entire Body's confession. The very act of the corporate confession is an explicit reminder that we are no better (or worse) than anyone else. We have all fallen short of the high calling to which we have been called. In a sense, our confession is an admission of the need for what Saint James, the brother of our Lord, writes to the Church: "Confess your sins to one another and pray for one another, so that you—*all of you*—may be healed."

Jesus says, "When two or three are gathered in my name, I am there." Jesus does not promise to be with us singularly, when we sit alone in our righteous anger and hold onto the heavy baggage we are tempted to carry. Rather, Jesus promises to be with us when we are in relationship—where two or three are gathered in his name, a name that means forgiveness and reconciliation.

The gospel is more than a policy and procedure manual for conflict resolution. It is a way of life defined by God's own relational nature as a trinity of persons—in perfect relationship and made known to us most clearly through Jesus Christ, who is himself the ultimate seeker of reconciliation among God's children.

We are called to love our neighbor as ourselves because we are called to live in relationship with a God who thrives on this very principle of communion in healthy relationships. We are called to offer forgiveness and seek reconciliation because God desires that his children will get along. Nobody said it was easy—but it is a better way to travel.

In the Church we are commanded to stop carrying our heavy baggage by letting go of our righteous anger and resentment right alongside our own sins and shortcomings. By doing so, we can more readily follow the way of Jesus Christ, by whom and with whom and in whom we have been reconciled and forgiven.

Reflecting on Our Story with God

❖ Try to remember a time you were locked out—literally or metaphorically—and you asked for and received what you needed to be restored.

❖ Reflect on the heavy baggage you have carried that belongs to you.

❖ Reflect on the heavy baggage you have carried that belongs to someone else.

Celebrating Our Story with God

❖ Imagine how you might forgive more readily and whether this may deepen your experience of the Lord's Prayer when you say "...forgive us our trespasses, as we forgive..."

❖ Offer thanks in prayer for various mercies of forgiveness you have received. If an expression of thanks to someone would be welcomed and well received, then also give written or verbal thanks to them too.

Chapter 10

Exchanging the Peace

Believe It or Not

Jesus said to them, "Peace be with you."

—Luke 24:36b

Now that we have set down the heavy baggage that gets in the way of healthy relationships with our neighbors, we are able to freely exchange the gift of peace and reconciliation with one another.

Jesus commands his followers not to approach the altar to meet God before being reconciled with one's neighbor (Matthew 5:23-24). Therefore, in the midst of Holy Eucharist, we practice what Jesus taught by proclaiming his peace with one another before we approach the altar.

In his letters to a church wrought with division and conflict (which means the letter is addressed to all churches

The Peace

All stand. The Celebrant says to the people

> The peace of the Lord be always with you.
>
> *People*   And also with you.

Then the Ministers and People may greet one another in the name of the Lord.

—The service for Holy Communion continues on page 360 of *The Book of Common Prayer.*

everywhere!), Saint John makes the case for reconciliation and peace, using a good dose of common sense:

> Those who say, "I love God," and hate their brothers or sisters are liars; for those who do not love a brother or sister whom they have seen, cannot love God whom they have not seen.
>
> —1 John 4:20

Therefore, the sacrament of Holy Communion must always include this essential and pivotal act of exchanging the peace of Christ. This is how we proclaim our reconciliation with one another so we can faithfully celebrate our communion—not only with God but also with one another. Put simply, there cannot be communion without the "union" part being fully in place.

The priest initiates the exchange of the peace by declaring, "The peace of the Lord be always with you." The people respond, "And also with you." At this point the congregation exchanges the gift of peace with one another. Some may restate the words, "the peace of the Lord" or "the peace of Christ" to people nearby. Others may simply offer the hand of friendship and a smile.

There is no single way to participate in this part of the liturgy. Some who have an informal sensibility may say "Good morning." Others may engage in a bit more of a conversation. The important point to remember is the depth of meaning found in this sacramental moment, regardless of how formal or informal one chooses to be in sharing the peace of Christ.

The exchange of the peace is central (both in meaning and sequence) within the celebration of Holy Eucharist. In some small parishes, every single worshiper has a chance to greet every other worshiper. In other congregations, the pause is brief and symbolic. In either case, we are following the way of Jesus, which is the way of peace.

In order to better understand the exchange of the peace, let's look at how graciously Jesus offered it.

> While the disciples were talking...Jesus himself stood among them and said to them, "Peace be with you." They were startled and terrified, and thought that they were seeing a ghost. He said to them, "Why are you frightened, and why do doubts arise in your hearts? Look at my hands and my feet; see that it is I myself. Touch me and see; for a ghost does not have flesh and bones as you see that I have." And when he had said this, he showed them his hands and his feet. While in their joy they were disbelieving and still wondering, he said to them, "Have you anything here to eat?" They gave him a piece of broiled fish, and he took it and ate in their presence.
>
> —Luke 24:36-43

According to this excerpt from Saint Luke, Jesus appears for the third time to his closest friends and followers with the unbelievably good news of his resurrection from the dead. And for the third time, they are only able to receive it as unbelievable news—not good news, just unbelievable news. Saint Luke helps all of us understand that disbelief is a normal reaction to Jesus' promise of resurrection as well as his delivery on that promise.

Bear in mind that we are not talking about the reaction of Jesus' enemies or skeptics who looked on from a distance. We are talking about Jesus' closest friends. We're talking about people like you and me. We're talking about people who have enough faith to show up despite questions and doubts, misgivings and fears. And still, the first reaction is doubt and disbelief.

†

A newly ordained pastor who was serving as an assistant under a wise and long-serving minister was suffering from a severe crisis of doubt, and he was despairing about what to do. It is not exactly easy dinner conversation for a newly ordained preacher to tell his supervising pastor that he doesn't think he believes in the resurrection. You can imagine the relief this young man experienced when the senior pastor assumed responsibility for preaching on Easter Sunday.

On Easter morning, the young cleric sat quietly with his profound doubts and watched as the wise preacher climbed into the pulpit. The elder priest stood, looked out at the congregation, and began his sermon: "You know, the disciples couldn't believe it either."

What would you give for the security of knowing everything will be okay? What would you pay your investment advisor, insurance agent, or banker for the certainty of your financial assets' safety? What would you pay your grocery store or the local water utility for the security of uncontaminated food and drink—despite the circumstances? What might you be willing to pay your favorite athletic program for the certainty of winning more games?

The disciples gather behind locked doors after Jesus' death because they feel insecure. They are uncertain about whether things are going to be okay. They huddle together, terrified about what might happen next. Into this den of fear walks Jesus, the risen Lord—unbelievable! At this pivotal moment, notice that Jesus does not offer them a gift of security but rather the gift of peace.

"Peace be with you!" Jesus says.

Now, peace and security can be compatible ideals, but they are by no means the same thing. The *Pax Romana* or "Peace of the Roman Empire" was only made possible because of the certainty that perceived troublemakers and disturbers of the status quo—like Jesus of Nazareth—would be brutally crucified and eliminated.

The Peace of Christ, on the other hand, is liberally available, even for his disbelieving followers. It is made possible through the faith and action of a merciful God who persistently blesses us with gifts we do not deserve.

Even after "three strikes" of disbelief, Jesus does not consider his disciples to have struck out. Jesus does not give up his faith in the disciples. Rather, he shows them the scars of his vulnerable body. Jesus invites his disbelieving friends to look and touch.

After all this, the disciples seem to have their fears relieved. Saint Luke reports that they were joyful…but they still couldn't believe the whole story. Nonetheless, Jesus invites his friends to gather around the table to share a meal of broiled fish, yet again. Jesus opens their minds to understand the scriptures, yet again. Jesus challenges them to be witnesses of his kind of peace and life, yet again.

As we prepare to gather around the altar table for our sacred meal, we exchange the gift of peace. We don't impose or force it, like the *Pax Romana*. We give and receive it as vulnerably as Christ did.

There is a misconception in twenty-first-century American culture that religion is all about belief. As we can see clearly from this story, belief has been a shortcoming ever since Jesus made his first appearances after the resurrection.

Yet, from those meager, unbelievable beginnings, Jesus has shown his disciples—us—what true religion is all about! True religion is about life, peaceable life with God and with one another.

If we wait until all our beliefs are neatly settled before we celebrate life in the peaceable way of Christ, we will never start. No matter what you believe about the details you heard in the Liturgy of the Word, it is time to proceed with the peaceable life of Christ. No matter what you believe about the details of faith and science, life and death, good and evil, it is time to proceed with the peaceable life of Christ that we celebrate with Holy Communion.

Earlier in this chapter, I quoted from the first letter of John about the importance of us being at peace with one another. John describes the gift of God's love in plain language anyone can understand. John sheds light on the essence of who we are created to be, even though we have not yet arrived at the fullness of this ideal.

In the midst of our questions and doubts, our divisions and conflicts, John nonetheless calls the Church through the gift of peace and reconciliation to participate even more deeply in the holy communion that God intends to share with God's children.

> See what love the Father has given us, that we should be called children of God, and that is what we are...Beloved, we are God's children now; what we will be has not yet been revealed. What we do know is this: when he is revealed, we will be like him, for we will see him as he is.
>
> —1 John 3:1-2

We worship a risen Lord who comes to us in peace, even when we are locked in fear. We follow a risen Lord who believes in us, even when we cannot believe in ourselves. We pray to a risen Lord who comes among us with healing and forgiveness, even when we cannot heal or forgive ourselves. We live in the fellowship of a risen Lord who seeks communion with us, even in our daily bread.

You and I are challenged to be witnesses of this kind of peace in word and deed. We are challenged to be witnesses of this kind of belief in spite of our doubts. We are challenged to be witnesses of Christ's healing and forgiveness through our prayers and our actions. We are challenged to be witnesses of his communion in our worship and in our fellowship.

In our Baptismal Covenant, we promise to be witnesses of these things. We promise to continue in the apostles' teaching and fellowship. We promise to continue in the breaking of bread and in the prayers.[viii]

We do these things because the disbelieving disciples did them. We do these things because we have learned that these are precisely the occasions when Jesus shows up in our lives, whether we believe it or not.

Reflecting on Our Story with God

❖ Think of a time when you craved certainty and instead received a gift of peace in spite of your fears or doubts.

❖ Reflect on the difference between a peace that is imposed or enforced and a peace that is freely offered as a gift. Which of these forms of peace is borne of strength? Which of these forms of peace requires vulnerability?

Celebrating Our Story with God

❖ Explore new and tangible ways you can offer the gift of peace "to those who are far off and those who are near" (Ephesians 2:17).

❖ Look around for images and narratives showing the gift of peace being freely exchanged. Consider what images or narratives of peace you might help depict or join—locally or globally.

Holy Communion

Chapter 11

The Offertory

Called Beyond Ourselves

With what shall I come before the Lord, and bow myself before God on high?
He has told you, O mortal, what is good; and what does the Lord require of
you but to do justice, and to love kindness, and to walk humbly with your God?

—Micah 6:6a, 8

The offertory signals the pivotal shift from the spoken and sung Liturgy of the Word to the second part of the service, sometimes called the Liturgy of the Table. This part of the service includes all the gifts of substance, tangible offerings of money, bread, and wine that can be physically placed upon an altar and set apart for the glory of God and the benefit of God's people. The offertory is the prerequisite moment during Holy Eucharist when these gifts are freely offered in order to become transformed for the benefit of Christ's continuing mission and ministry in the world.

The Holy Communion

The Celebrant may begin the Offertory with one of the sentences on page 376, or with some other sentence of Scripture.

During the Offertory, a hymn, psalm, or anthem may be sung.

Representatives of the congregation bring the people's offerings of bread and wine, and money or other gifts, to the deacon or celebrant. The people stand while the offerings are presented and placed on the Altar.

—The service for Holy Communion continues on page 361 of *The Book of Common Prayer*.

Yet, the money, bread, and wine are not the first gifts we have offered to God in our celebration of the Holy Eucharist. Our first offering was the prayers of the people, when we gave up the deepest needs and desires of our hearts over which we have no control.

Second, we offered our confession—the thing over which we have some marginal control but still hinges mostly on God's (and our neighbor's) willingness to forgive. Third, we offered the peace of Christ—the gift over which we have mutual control. This offering is fully realized only when we share it with one another.

The offertory then is the culmination of all these offerings. Having already given up to God's mercy the things over which we have no or only marginal control and sharing the gift of peace over which we have mutual control, we now have the opportunity to give the thing over which we have total control. At last, we have the chance to offer our power.

That's right! The offertory is about much more than a collection of money. This is the sacred moment when we boldly proclaim our power to make a difference in God's name.

Money is the most conspicuous symbol of our power—it supports the ability to make choices in our lives and in the lives of others. Money is simply the tool we use to measure and use this power. When we spend money, we show the world how we choose to *use* our power. When we give away money, we show the world how we choose to *share* our power. Accordingly, we can discover great freedom by letting go of some of our power—as Christ did in even more drastic ways—for the glory of God and the benefit of others.

In exercising this freedom, we have the chance to participate in a divine mission that is larger than our own private projects and goals. In choosing to be generous, we have the chance to live according to the divine pattern of life.

The prophet Micah summarizes this divine pattern as a basic, attainable requirement—to use our power and money to do justice, love kindness (also known as mercy), and to walk humbly with our God. The most direct pathway to walking with humility and practicing justice and mercy is to be generous with our power.

Generosity is a virtue at all times and in all places and especially in the celebration of Holy Communion when our gifts are held up alongside the greatest gift of all—the gift of Jesus Christ. In this context, our gifts are offered by him and with him and in him. In fact, this becomes a tangible reality when the ushers (or others) bring forward both the monetary offerings given by the people as well as gifts of the bread and wine that will be used for the sacrament of Holy Communion.

Our sacrifice of praise and thanksgiving mingles with the divine gifts of justice, mercy, and humility. Our sacrifice of praise and thanksgiving prepares us to receive the gift of Holy Communion for what it is—God's power shared with us.

Jesus has a lot to say about generosity. One of his demanding teachings occurs when he meets a rich young man on a journey.

As he was setting out on a journey, a man ran up and knelt before Jesus, and asked him, "Good Teacher, what must I do to inherit eternal life?" Jesus said to him, "Why do you call me good? No one is good but God alone. You know the commandments: You shall not murder; You shall not commit adultery; You shall not steal; You shall not bear false witness; You shall not defraud; Honor your father and mother." He said to Jesus, "Teacher, I have kept all these since my youth." Jesus, looking at him, loved him and said, "You lack one thing; go, sell what you own, and give the money to the poor, and you will have treasure in heaven; then come, follow me." When he heard this, he was shocked and went away grieving, for he had many possessions.

Then Jesus looked around and said to his disciples, "How hard it will be for those who have wealth to enter the kingdom of God!" And the disciples were perplexed at these words. But Jesus said to them again, "Children, how hard it is to enter the kingdom of God! It is easier for a camel to go through the eye of a needle than for someone who is rich to enter the kingdom of God." They were greatly astounded and said to one another, "Then who can be saved?" Jesus looked at them and said, "For mortals it is impossible, but not for God; for God all things are possible."

—Mark 10:17-27

This passage from the Gospel according to Saint Mark reveals the crux of what the offertory is all about. A young man runs up to Jesus, knowing what he wants to receive—eternal life. Yet he has not considered all that he has available to give.

He wants to inherit God's mercy for himself without ever having appreciated how much God is blessed by the mercy we share with others. In the offertory as well as in the gospel, the gifts we share help prepare us to be fully thankful for the gifts God shares with us. Giving away some of our power helps open up room in our hearts to receive and be thankful for the power God is willing to give us.

I'm sure we all can think of examples of everyday gifts and mercies for which we are thankful—as well as everyday offerings that we have shared for the benefit of others. I will never forget my experience of receiving an extraordinary gift offered by a stranger.

†

In 1988, a year before a half million Chinese people converged on Tiananmen Square in Beijing to protest for reform, I received a miraculous gift. It was one year before a single, unarmed man inspired the world by facing down an army tank, stubbornly refusing to back down as he cried out for justice.

As part of my journey around the world during college, I visited China. Sitting with a dozen other foreigners in a youth hostel dormitory, I repacked my backpack under the pale green hue of a fluorescent light. We were setting out in search of the buses and trains to carry us along our journeys throughout this huge and immensely populated country.

A young Canadian was leaning over her backpack nearby, struggling to close the zipper in time to catch the next bus out of town. This was not an unusual sight: Backpackers are constantly discerning what to keep and what to discard or give away in order to travel without too much weight. What caught my eye, though, was when she tore a thick paperback novel in half along the book's spine.

"What's that?" I asked.

"*Les Misérables* by Victor Hugo," she replied.

"You know, it's probably an unpardonable sin to destroy a book that spectacular," I said with a smile, "unless…*unless* you were willing to give those pages to me!" I was teasing her of course. Yet, as I looked at the cover of that Penguin paperback, I thought perhaps the discarded 700 pages could keep me company for the next couple of months, and I could simply buy the book when I returned home in order to finish reading the novel.

She handed me the chunk of pages. And this small, yet significant gift changed my life.

I had attended the musical *Les Misérables* more than once. I had heard the story of those miserable souls enduring the unjust and unrighteous state of affairs in nineteenth-century France—*les misérables* who cried out for justice.

And yet I was not prepared for how powerfully Hugo's words would affect me. He spoke to me like a prophet, challenging my own power and privilege, challenging my own abhorrence of those who stubbornly refuse to back down or step aside. Those 700 pages confronted me just as Jesus had confronted a rich, young man in his own day.

Like the young man in the gospel, I followed the rules, and I stayed out of trouble. Yet, Jesus says following the rules and staying out of trouble is not enough.

Jesus calls the rich young man to be generous. Jesus still calls the rich to be generous. Jesus still calls us to be generous.

Like that young Canadian woman who handed me those pages, we are at least called to give away the surplus we don't need for our journey, to hand off excessive possessions that weigh us down.

I don't believe Jesus calls everyone to sell everything in order to follow him, even though that's what he tells the man in the passage from Mark. But I believe Jesus calls us to a level of generosity that most of us consider beyond our reach: Radical generosity and discipleship often seem impossible to people like us, mere mortals.

Jesus says, "For mortals it is impossible, but not for God; for God all things are possible!" If we truly believe that promise and trust in it, then we will be inspired to open wide our hands and our hearts with a miraculous generosity that changes lives.

We are called to give because God gives. And with God, all things are possible. We are called to bless because God blesses. And with God, all things are possible. We are challenged to respond generously and proportionally with the gifts God has given us.

I spent the next two months traveling all over China—having entered from Hong Kong, traveling west as far as the Old Burma Road, north as far as Inner Mongolia, and concluding in Beijing. Translating, it would be like starting in South Carolina, going to New Orleans, moving north to Chicago, and finishing in New York City. All the while, I devoured the pages of *Les Misérables*.

Although I am a slow reader, I moved through those 700 pages at an unprecedented pace. This small, yet significant gift was changing my life, and I was grateful. The words helped sustain me through the most demanding parts of my journey. As I read each night, sometimes by flashlight, I began to realize I would finish the first half well before I returned home.

Two thousand miles after receiving the first half of the book, I arrived in one of the most populated cities in the world. The sidewalk in Beijing overflowed with people, a chaotic swirl of pedestrians and bicycles. And then I saw her: the Canadian woman whose small, yet significant gift had begun transforming my life.

I made my way through the crowd and shouted to her. "This book is unbelievable!" I said. "I must get the second half from you as soon as you finish! There is no way I can wait until I get back home to purchase the remainder."

Fortunately, she had just finished reading the book. We agreed to meet at the same corner the next afternoon so she could give me the second half of *Les Misérables*.

In the gospel story of Jesus and the rich, young man, Jesus is setting out on a journey when the man runs up and asks what he must do to inherit eternal life.

We need to remember an important point: Eternal life is not a destination; it is a journey. Eternal life is a way of life defined by incredible and miraculous generosity. It is a journey in which we are sustained by gifts that transform our lives and during which we have the power to offer gifts that transform other peoples' lives.

Sometimes, this seems impossible. We are tempted like the rich, young man in the gospel to back down or step aside, unwilling to give up all the possessions we hold dear. Yet the gospel is clear. When we journey with Jesus—when we follow Jesus without hesitation or counting the cost—miracles happen, and lives transform.

At the offertory of the Holy Eucharist, we have the chance to offer gifts for the sake of justice, kindness, and humility. It is a special opportunity for us to offer our power to make a difference in other people's lives and in our own. Where else in our lives can we mingle our perhaps small, but significant gifts with God's greatest gift in order to make a difference in the world?

Right in the middle of God's gift of Holy Communion we are called—like the rich, young man is called by Jesus—to move beyond our doubts and our fears and become generous *with* God. We are called beyond what we believe is impossible with the promise that with God, *all things are possible.*

The miraculous and transforming gift I received in 1988 through a stranger's generosity across 2,000 miles and two months of travel is an example in my life of how I have learned that with God, all things are possible. Maybe the promise of God's miraculous possibility mingled with our generosity yields the most surprising and transforming gifts of all!

Reflecting on Our Story with God

❖ Think of times when you were surprised, or even transformed, by someone's generosity.

❖ Can you remember a time when you felt particularly challenged by Christ's call to be generous? In what ways did your response open up new, miraculous, and transforming possibilities for others?

❖ Imagine your offering during the celebration of Holy Communion as your own holy thanks-giving, one that mingles with the gifts of God to become a source of power for justice, kindness, and humility.

Celebrating Our Story with God

❖ Consider an anonymous gift of an especially transforming book, song, or movie to someone who might experience it in the same way.

❖ Write a note to someone from your past who gave you a gift you still use or value. Even if you thanked the person when you first received it, imagine what it would feel like to hear of your ongoing and enduring gratitude years later.

Chapter 12

The Great Thanksgiving

Giving Up and Giving Thanks

O Give thanks to the Lord for he is good; for his steadfast love endures forever.

—1 Chronicles 16:34

After all of the offerings we make, exchange, and share during the Liturgy of the Word, something even more special happens during the Liturgy of the Table. In this second part of the celebration, God offers a gift to us. The gift of Holy Communion includes the forgiveness of sins, strength in our weakness, and everlasting salvation through Jesus Christ our Lord.

In this chapter we will look at the Great Thanksgiving in its entirety as a comprehensive prayer, before subsequently

The Great Thanksgiving

Alternative forms will be found on page 367 and following.

—The service for Holy Communion continues
with Eucharistic Prayer A on page 361
of *The Book of Common Prayer.*

exploring more carefully some of the components that make up this expression of our gratitude for the gifts of God. In fact, there are four versions of the Great Thanksgiving in *The Book of Common Prayer*: Eucharistic Prayer A, B, C, and D. They all begin and end pretty much the same, but noteworthy differences in the middle distinguish them as particularly appropriate for different seasons of the church year. These prayers begin on pages 361, 367, 369, and 372 respectively.

All sorts of events—religious and secular—make room for memorializing people, events, or places. These events can help us contend with sadness and grief. Even more events in our triumphalist culture celebrate joy, happiness, team spirit, and victory. One of the spectacular miracles of Holy Communion is that it is the only event in the world that can respect, bless, and even hallow (make holy) the deepest sadness within one person and the greatest joy within another person, standing side by side at the same time.

In an age when more people seem to be drifting away from the church, one of the unfortunate consequences for them (and for all of us) is that there are more empty spots around the only table in our culture that honors everyone, no matter who they are or how they are feeling. This table has room not only for those who rejoice but also for those who weep. This hallowed space blesses all these people *together* at the very same time.

One of my special memories is recalling how my large family would come together around the table at Thanksgiving. Being the youngest in my family (by a long shot), I was still a boy when my sisters married and began having children.

My mother prepared a feast for three generations. With young children around, not everyone was happy all the time. Yet everyone was welcomed and included. This is the table where I first recognized the importance of everyone receiving and sharing a blessing, together, at the same time.

One of the spiritual risks all people face, whether they consider themselves to be religious or not, is focusing too much on success, often to the exclusion or subjugation of others. The ideal of success permeates our lives. "Winners" appear conspicuously in our favorite movies, television shows, and books. Unparalleled, overwhelming success is the paragon of business, athletics, and every other enterprise (including religious ones) in our world.

The danger is that we can become so inclined toward winning—spiritually and otherwise—that we squeeze out room around the table for those who are losing and those who are lost.

When we identify ourselves with spiritual winners, we are tempted to hold tightly to the good deeds and accomplishments that have gotten us to where we are and then play them out before God like trump cards or try to cash them in like chips. The Wisdom of Sirach from the Old Testament calls winners up short. Sirach teaches us to practice a humble prayer of giving up, not an opportunistic prayer of trading up.

"Give to the Most High as he has given to you, and as generously as you can afford. [But] do not offer him a bribe, for he will not accept it."

—Sirach 35:12, 14

When we identify ourselves with spiritual losers, we desperately hope for an economy of grace because we know we cannot earn God's favor based on our merit. A calculus based on winners and losers fails to acknowledge that sometimes we will feel so defeated that there are no chips to turn in for God's blessing. There are times when our needs are beyond our control, and we have no leverage to negotiate for God's mercy. In these situations, all we can do is give up. But Jesus turns giving up upside down, seeing it as a blessed occasion, a humble moment before we become justified—set right—with God.

It is fitting, therefore, that we begin the Great Thanksgiving prayer by giving up our hearts. Giving up is the only way that both winners and losers can approach the gift of Holy Communion. For those who rejoice as well as those who weep, giving up is how we give thanks.

The priest invites us to do this by saying, "Lift up your hearts." And we reply, "We lift them to the Lord," which is just another way of saying, "We give them up to the Lord."

We have given up our prayers, our confession, and our offerings, and now with the giving up of our hearts, we are prepared to give thanks to God from whom all blessings flow.

†

After many years away from my hometown, I returned to attend a funeral for someone who had died tragically. It was a day to give up. It was a day to give up to God someone who was well loved. It was a day to give up to God our broken hearts and to pray, "Lord, have mercy."

I arrived in town early for the funeral. This almost never happens because I am generally trying to squeeze in as many things in a day as I can. Arriving early turned out to be a blessed occasion; I did not realize how much I needed to give up. For an hour or so before the funeral, I experienced a humble and quiet time of prayer at my boyhood home.

I walked around the yard where I used to cut grass for hours and hours in the blazing summer heat—a good deed if ever there was one. Someone else is taking good care of that yard now. In a quiet moment, I gave it up, and I gave thanks to God for having been challenged by a task that demanded my best effort.

I ran my finger down into the deep crevices of bark on a Loblolly Pine. It was so much wider and taller than I remembered. The roots had grown deep, and the branches had spread wide. The place where I put down roots had changed a lot over the years. In a quiet moment, I gave it up, and I gave thanks to God for having a good place to grow up myself.

As it turns out, there is not a big difference between giving up and giving thanks because both of these prayers require us to look beyond ourselves. Both of these prayers force us to look beyond our accomplishments, our resources, and our good deeds.

Both of these prayers challenge us to surrender our sense of entitlement about what we deserve or what we have earned. Both of these prayers challenge us to rely upon the grace and mercy of God, the great lover of humble souls who are giving up and giving thanks.

Giving up does not mean being lazy or failing to realize our full, God-given potential. Giving up simply means realizing that God is not as impressed with our accomplishments as we are. Giving up means realizing that *God* is God, and we are not.

The New Testament shares a personal letter Saint Paul wrote to Timothy, a trusted companion. Paul offers his best, retrospective counsel to the young man: "I have fought the good fight, I have finished the race, I have kept the faith." (2 Timothy 4:7)

In other words, Paul is giving up and giving thanks. He is recognizing the limits of his accomplishments and giving them up as a gift—not a bribe or a card or a chip—but a simple gift to our merciful God.

Win, lose, or draw, there is one place in life where all are welcomed to gather and be blessed. We may not have said or done all the right things before we arrived at Holy Eucharist. We may have experienced rousing success or utter failure. Yet when we come to the table for communion, at that moment when we give up and give thanks, our souls discover the fluency of a sincere prayer that draws us toward the gifts of God.

In the celebration of Holy Communion, we experience the blessing of gifts being transformed in our very midst. Offerings of prayer and confession are transformed into gifts of mercy and forgiveness. Offerings of power become united in a common mission of compassion and abundance. Giving up and giving thanks brings us face to face with the outward and visible signs of God's gift—inward and spiritual grace *for life.*

Holy Communion is a journey of transformation, and all are invited. It leads us to the place we need to gather but cannot find on our own. We arrive empty-handed with nothing to give—no bribe to offer, no cards to play, no chips to cash in.

We come to the table with nothing but gratitude as we reach out our hands to receive what we need and cannot give ourselves: the grace and strength of God's love communicated through the life of Christ by the power of the Holy Spirit.

And so we give thanks to our gracious and merciful God who uses the gift of Holy Communion to transform us into "living members of the body of his Son and heirs of God's eternal kingdom."[ix]

There is no better place in the world to experience the respect, blessing, and honor that is equally bestowed upon the sad and the joyful, the lost and the found, the weak and the strong. There is no safer place in the world to give up and give thanks.

Reflecting on Our Story with God

❖ Reflect on the difficult and blessed occasions when you have given up before God.

❖ Try to remember a time when you let go of a chip you held tightly in hopes of trading up with God and stood empty-handed and vulnerable, with nothing but the words, "Lord, have mercy," rolling off your lips.

❖ Think of some of the important tables in your life—at home, in the church, or elsewhere—where you have experienced the blessing of receiving grace and love, together with others, at the same time.

Celebrating Our Story with God

❖ Consider visiting a place—physically or spiritually—where you may still have things you need to give up and for which you need to give thanks.

❖ The next time you attend Holy Eucharist, cultivate your awareness of the emotional breadth of experience in the room. Give thanks for a safe place where the lost and the found can be with God just as they are and at the same time.

Chapter 13

The Eucharistic Prayer

Do This in Remembrance

While they were eating, Jesus took a loaf of bread, and after blessing it he broke it, and gave it to the disciples.

—Matthew 26:26

In the last chapter we looked broadly at the Great Thanksgiving as a whole and how this prayer invites the gathered community to give up and give thanks as the prerequisite, faithful preparation for receiving the gifts of God. In this chapter we will focus more narrowly on the basic elements of the Great Thanksgiving, which can be found in each of the four eucharistic prayers—A, B, C, and D. These basic elements include the *Sursum Corda*, the *Sanctus*, the Institution Narrative, the Memorial Acclamation, the *Epiclesis*, and the great AMEN. Although the particular words and the order of these elements may differ somewhat from one eucharistic prayer to another, each is always present in the celebration. (The following examples are all taken from Eucharistic Prayer A, which begins on page 361 of *The Book of Common Prayer.*)

Sursum Corda

Eucharistic Prayer A

The people remain standing. The Celebrant, whether bishop or priest, faces them and sings or says

	The Lord be with you.
People	And also with you.
Celebrant	Lift up your hearts.
People	We lift them to the Lord.
Celebrant	Let us give thanks to the Lord our God.
People	It is right to give him thanks and praise.

Then, facing the Holy Table, the Celebrant proceeds

It is right, and a good and joyful thing, always and everywhere to give thanks to you, Father Almighty, Creator of heaven and earth.

—The service for Holy Communion continues on page 361 of *The Book of Common Prayer.*

Sursum Corda is a Latin phrase that translates, "Lift up your hearts." As described in the previous chapter, these are the first words of invitation from the priest to the people as we begin celebrating our thanksgiving.

We will discuss in a later chapter the centuries-old debate about whether the bread and wine literally become Jesus' body and blood. Within the Anglican tradition, people have various positions on this, but for our discussion now, the words of Thomas Cranmer, author of the first Anglican prayer book and Queen Elizabeth's Archbishop of Canterbury, express a fundamental and incontrovertible belief: What happens in the eucharist occurs because our hearts are lifted heavenward.

In our present age when there is a compulsive, cultural emphasis on convenience, we need to be honest about the fact that whatever happens in the Holy Eucharist, it is not convenient—nor is it routine. Rather, we are celebrating an awe-inspiring sacrifice—one that we mark with praise and thanksgiving by pausing in our lives to lift up our hearts to God. We must be willing to still our demands for our needs and wants so that we are available for blessing, healing, forgiveness, and abundance that come through the eucharist.

We all need a regular infusion of God's love in order to be healthy and vibrant. But some of us may need a transplant— a change of heart—in order to reclaim the abundant life that God intends for God's children. Both of these gifts are promised in holy scripture.

In the Letter to the Hebrews, the author urges people to approach God with a true heart in full assurance because God is faithful (Hebrews 10:22). In other words, we can trust the source of the lifeblood we need.

In the Old Testament prophesy of Ezekiel, long before there was a medical idea of open-heart surgery, the prophet expressed the promise of God this way: "A new heart I will give you, and a new spirit I will put within you; and I will remove from your body the heart of stone and give you a heart of flesh" (Ezekiel 36:26).

Any cardiac patient will tell you that nothing in the world is less convenient or routine yet necessary than infusion of new blood or even a new heart. It is a life-giving interruption for the recipient—and a life-saving gift by the donor.

And so it is with the gift of Holy Communion. Since the night before Jesus' life is interrupted and sacrificed for the sake of love, Holy Communion has been the chosen vessel to deliver God's grace to our hearts. Jesus himself makes it clear when he says, "Do *this* in remembrance of me."

The love of God is a heartbeat away, and yet God does not force it upon us. We must be willing recipients who open our hearts and lift them up to receive the gift we need for life.

Sanctus

Celebrant and People

Holy, holy, holy Lord, God of power and might,
heaven and earth are full of your glory.
    Hosanna in the highest.
Blessed is he who comes in the name of the Lord.
    Hosanna in the highest.

Sanctus is the Latin word for holy. When we sing the *Sanctus*, we are rejoicing in the holiness of God. The lyrics and musical settings have several variations but perhaps the most common is the rendering that appears above.

Isaiah, the Old Testament prophet, describes an exquisite vision of God's holiness.

> In the year King Uzziah died, I saw the Lord sitting on a throne, high and lofty; and the hem of his robe filled the temple. Seraphs were in attendance above him; each had six wings: with two they covered their faces, and with two they covered their feet, and with two they flew. And one called to another and said: "Holy, holy, holy is the Lord of hosts; the whole earth is full of his glory."
>
> —Isaiah 6:1-3

We believe this reverent prayer is so important that it gets included in every celebration of Holy Eucharist: "Holy, Holy, Holy; Lord God of Hosts: Heaven and earth are full of your glory."

When we behold the holiness of God, there is but one response—to bow down with reverence before the Lord. After the priest first uses lifted hands during the *Sursum Corda* to invite the people to "Lift up your hearts," the next posture of prayer is to bow one's head—at least symbolically—in reverence of God's holiness at the beginning of the *Sanctus*.

Isaiah is not the only one to receive the gift of seeing holiness. In the Revelation to Saint John, we hear his testimony about holiness. "After this, I looked and there in heaven a door stood open!" (4:1). Once again, the lesson describes a vision— something that could be seen. This awe-inspiring vision was an invitation for Saint John the Divine to enter and participate in worship.

The origins of the *Sanctus* belong to Isaiah, and the Book of Revelation bids us to join with prophets, apostles, martyrs, one another, and all the company of heaven to worship God's holiness.

And—this detail is really important—we gather *around* our God who is at the center of our common life. The God who creates, redeems, and sustains this holy, holy, holy communion of saints, living and dead, is the one and only center of our eternal worship.

There is a paradox at the heart of our *Sanctus* prayer. God's holiness—otherness, set apartness, transcendence—is true precisely because of God's miraculous nearness, central presence, and immanence. And so we sing and speak our worship and adoration, not solving the mystery but beholding it nonetheless and entering it, just like Isaiah and Saint John, with reverence and awe.

Another part of the *Sanctus* is also worthy of our attention. We sing, "Blessed is he who comes in the name of the Lord. Hosanna in the highest!" This refrain is taken from the story of Jesus' triumphal arrival in Jerusalem near the end of his life (Matthew 21:9).

As Jesus enters Jerusalem, riding on the colt of a donkey, multitudes of people spread palm branches and cloaks along the road and shouts these words in adoration and worship. Yet, we know just how quickly joy and praise turned into fear and cursing. On Palm Sunday, we pray to God for the courage to "walk in the way of Christ's suffering, and also share in his resurrection."[x]

Institution Narrative

The people stand or kneel.

Then the Celebrant continues

Holy and gracious Father: In your infinite love you made us for yourself; and, when we had fallen into sin and become subject to evil and death, you, in your mercy, sent Jesus Christ, your only and eternal Son, to share our human nature, to live and die as one of us, to reconcile us to you, the God and Father of all.

He stretched out his arms upon the cross, and offered himself in obedience to your will, a perfect sacrifice for the whole world.

At the following words concerning the bread, the Celebrant is to hold it or lay a hand upon it; and at the words concerning the cup, to hold or place a hand upon the cup and any other vessel containing wine to be consecrated.

On the night he was handed over to suffering and death, our Lord Jesus Christ took bread; and when he had given thanks to you, he broke it, and gave it to his disciples, and said, "Take, eat: This is my Body, which is given for you. Do this for the remembrance of me."

After supper he took the cup of wine; and when he had given thanks, he gave it to them, and said, "Drink this, all of you: This is my Blood of the new Covenant, which is shed for you and for many for the forgiveness of sins. Whenever you drink it, do this for the remembrance of me."

As we move into the Institution Narrative, we recognize that Jesus did not enter into glory until after he suffered and died. In other words, we acknowledge that the way of Jesus is a walk in the way of his cursed suffering with assurance that we also share in his blessed resurrection. We proclaim that the blessed and cursed body that Christ gave to be broken becomes the gift of God for the people of God. It sets the stage for us to receive this gift in remembrance that Christ died for us and to feed on him in our hearts by faith, with thanksgiving.[xi]

The eucharistic prayer continues with our remembrance of how God created the human family in God's own image and invited us to live with perfect freedom and peace. Our story includes God's never-failing love—and those times when we failed in this high calling.

In Eucharistic Prayer B we specifically remember the gifts of covenant, freedom, the law, and the prophets by which we are empowered to live well with God and our neighbors. Above all, we remember the gift of Jesus who triumphed over evil and death and opened the way to eternal life.

Finally, we remember the special occasion when Jesus *took* bread, *gave thanks* (*eucharisteo*), *broke* it, and *gave* it to his disciples as an outward and visible sign of his sacrificial gift of love. He also did the same with the cup.

Let me share a lesson about sacrifice that involves the four-fold actions of taking and blessing, breaking and giving. I found them in a booklet written by a chaplain to help people recognize and remember these patterns in our worship and in our lives.[xii]

In ancient Hebrew practice, the person offering a sacrifice would *take* an animal and present it to the priest. Second, he would *lay his hands on it*—personally designating the animal to represent him in the sacrifice. Next, the animal would be *killed*. And by virtue of this sacrifice, it would serve as a propitiating act of *giving* over one's sins (or thanksgiving) to God.

Now, notice how the gospels describe this same four-fold pattern with regard to the passion of Jesus Christ. He is *taken* before Pilate. The soldiers *lay hands on him*. His body is *destroyed*. And ultimately, through his resurrection, we discover the *giving* of new and transformed life.

This four-step pattern unfolds every time we celebrate the Holy Eucharist. On behalf of everyone present, the priest *takes* the bread and wine that the people bring forward along with our other offerings. The priest *lays hands upon it* and *blesses it*. Then the priest *breaks* it, recalling how Christ—our Passover—is sacrificed for us. And then the action is completed when the priest *gives back* what was taken, blessed, and broken.

We worship a God who transforms what is *taken* into gifts that can be *given*. We worship a God who transforms what is *broken* into possibilities for blessing.

Working with our creativity, God miraculously enables crushed wheat to become life-giving bread, which we receive as the gift of Christ's Body. Working with our creativity, God miraculously enables crushed grapes to become life-giving wine, which we receive as the gift of Christ's Blood.

Even more miraculously, God is willing to take us—broken as we are—and transform us into a blessing, which is given and shared.

When we celebrate the Holy Eucharist, we re-enact this pattern that began with the Hebrews and was made manifest through Jesus. We remember this pattern in our worship so that we can recognize it in our own lives as God continues to work miracles of transformation within us.

Thus far, the eucharistic prayer has emphasized remembering God's love from the past as we have discovered it through the holy scriptures of the Old and New Testaments. After lifting up our hearts in the *Sursum Corda* and bowing with reverence during the *Sanctus*, we have been remembering the story of God's love through history and particularly through Jesus Christ.

Memorial Acclamation

Therefore we proclaim the mystery of faith:

Celebrant and People

Christ has died.
Christ is risen.
Christ will come again.

Next comes a moment where everyone gets the chance to acclaim the truth, goodness, and beauty of God's love story—not only in the past but also in the present and for the future. The Memorial Acclamation is spoken by everyone. All of us proclaim the reality of God's eternal love—past, present, and future. We say together: "Christ *has* died. Christ *is* risen. Christ *will* come again" (Eucharistic Prayer A). The same fullness is expressed in Eucharistic Prayer B: "We remember his death (in the past); we proclaim his resurrection (in the present); and we await his coming in glory (in the future)."

Acclaiming our memory of Christ—*alpha and omega*, beginning and end—is a perfect summary of our trust in God's eternal, living, and loving presence throughout history, no matter what. Despite the worst possible response to God that we could muster (crucifixion), the Father's eternal, loving purpose could not be frustrated. Indeed, through Christ, our worst is transformed into God's best.

And so we acclaim the One who was, and is, and is to come. We acclaim the One who sits upon the throne at the right hand of the Father. We acclaim him as worthy to receive glory and honor, thanksgiving and blessing, now and forever.[xiii]

Epiclesis

Sanctify them by your Holy Spirit to be for your people the Body and Blood of your Son, the holy food and drink of new and unending life in him. Sanctify us also that we may faithfully receive this holy Sacrament, and serve you in unity, constancy, and peace; and at the last day bring us with all your saints into the joy of your eternal kingdom.

Up until this point, the eucharistic prayer has recounted extensively the story of God's love offered by the Father and through the Son. References to the third person of the Trinity—the Holy Spirit—have been sparse, if not altogether absent.

This reminds me of a comment by the Roman Catholic cardinal Walter Kasper that may sound a little sacrilegious until you realize it is not a comment about God but rather about *us*. He said, "The Holy Spirit is the Cinderella of the Trinity. All the work, none of the credit!" This reflects a familiar pattern in theological writings and devotionals throughout the history of the church and particularly in the Western Hemisphere. Even in the Nicene Creed from the year 325, which we still affirm, the Holy Spirit seems somewhat inferior as the only member of the Trinity that proceeds *from* the other two.

Before Jesus leaves his disciples and ascends into heaven, he promises they are not being left alone. In the closing words in the Gospel according to Saint Matthew, Jesus says, "Remember, I am with you always, to the end of the age." In the Gospel according to Saint John, Jesus assures his disciples, "When the *parakletos*[xiv] comes, whom I will send to you from the Father...he will testify on my behalf" (John 15:26).

Many modern versions of the Bible translate this Greek word *parakletos* as advocate, counselor, comforter, or helper because we associate these roles with God's Holy Spirit. The translation of *parakletos* is "One called beside." Notice the parts of this compound word: *para*—beside, as in parallel lines, and *kletos*—called. If you think of this in a legal context, the one who is called to stand beside a defendant in a courtroom is an "advocate" or "counselor." In a less formal, more pastoral setting, we can see that one who is called to stand beside another is a "comforter."

Notice how Jesus promises God's own loving, life-giving presence can be summoned by us to stand beside us so that we are not alone. By the power of the Holy Spirit, God's love and life are with us always, even to the end of the age.

Now we can get back to looking at that other Greek word for what happens at this moment in the Holy Eucharist—the *epiclesis*. *Paraklesis* means called beside; *epiclesis* means called upon.

Let's look at the words in Eucharistic Prayer B from *The Book of Common Prayer* (page 369). "We pray you, Gracious God, to send your Holy Spirit *upon* these gifts that they may be the Sacrament of the Body of Christ and his Blood of the new Covenant. Unite us to your Son in his sacrifice, that we may be acceptable through him, being sanctified by the Holy Spirit."

At this point in the prayer, we present back to God the simple gifts of bread and wine, and we pray for God's loving, life-giving presence to be with us. We call upon God's Holy Spirit to transform the gifts *and us* so that we might be blessed and strengthened as outward and visible signs of God's love.

God's Holy Spirit—the perfect love between the Father and the Son and us—is our *parakletos*, called beside us as advocate, counselor, comforter, and helper. God's Spirit is alive and in love with the children of God and the gifts of God. The good news is that we are not left alone. God's presence is with us to the end of the age.

AMEN!

All this we ask through your Son Jesus Christ. By him, and with him, and in him, in the unity of the Holy Spirit all honor and glory is yours, Almighty Father, now and for ever. AMEN.

The most powerless person in the world is a priest. The vocation of a priest is—in simple terms—to represent God to the people and the people to God. Thus, without the people, there is really no use for the priest.

God does not require people to have an "agent," but it has proven useful throughout history for at least one member of a community to have particular responsibility for studying, interpreting, preaching, teaching, and celebrating God's presence and promise for the people.

A priest's job is to pray for people. A priest's job is also to pray with people and to lead them in practicing the discipline of discovering, celebrating, and sharing the love of God themselves.

I once was asked by a member of the altar guild early one Sunday morning to bless some water so she could fill the baptismal font. Many parishioners dip their finger in the font and make the sign of the cross as a reminder of their baptism when they enter the church.

I explained that I couldn't bless the water by myself. A priest cannot pronounce a blessing alone. We require the presence of at least one other person in honor of Jesus' teaching that where two or more are gathered, Christ is present. In other words, the priest can pray but someone else must be around to say, "Amen." Most people have heard or said this word without really thinking about the definition. Its meaning is deceptively simple: "So be it, may it ever be so, I concur, or right on," depending upon your vernacular.

The altar guild member paused her errands and stood beside me as I prayed that the water might be a sign of the cleansing and refreshment of God's grace. "Amen," she said, ratifying my prayer by affirming her hope and expectation that "may it be so" that God continue to use simple things like water, bread, and wine to communicate important truths.

In the celebration of Holy Communion, priests have the privilege of praying the Great Thanksgiving on behalf of the congregation, in part because it would be unwieldy and distracting for lots of people to speak this entire prayer in unison. However, priests do not get to say our own "Amen." Affirming the prayer is the privilege and responsibility of the congregation. Without the congregation's concurrence with the prayer, it is nothing more than a private devotion witnessed by people who do not agree.

Technically speaking, if the congregation fails to respond with "Amen," the priest should wait or start again. I once celebrated the Holy Eucharist with a small, quiet, and shy congregation in a chapel. They followed along attentively and faithfully as I prayed, but at the conclusion of the eucharistic prayer, nobody spoke up and said amen. (In *The Book of Common Prayer*, this word is so important that the publishers italicize and put it in all caps!) I stood still and smiled, gesturing with my hands that it was their turn to speak and say, "so be it!" They did, and we continued the celebration.

Do This in Remembrance

All the members of the gathered community lift up their hearts in anticipation of God's blessing. The gathered community bows in reverence as faithful people have done since the thresholds shook for the prophet Isaiah. The gathered community remembers and acclaims the loving acts of God—Father, Son, and Holy Spirit—in the past, in the present, and for the future. And, finally, the people of God affirm this celebration of our thanksgiving as real and true.

Research has shown that we remember 10 percent of what we read, 20 percent of what we hear, 30 percent of what we see, and 80 percent of what we personally experience. Therefore, we should understand why it is so important for us to *do this* in remembrance of Christ.

It is not enough to read about it, hear about it, or see it performed by others. There is just no substitute for honoring and remembering Christ than to do this in remembrance. Jesus himself selected this as the central vessel for helping us when, above all other options, he said, "Do this in remembrance of me."

Our personal experience of Holy Communion is essential to remembering the One to whom we belong. There is no other occasion quite like the eucharist, as people in all their diversity are re-membered—re-connected—with God and one another as living members of the Body. So be it. *AMEN!*

Reflecting on and Celebrating
Our Story with God

❖ *Sursum Corda*—Reflect on the interruptions and sacrifices you have experienced in life that have given you "lifeblood" or a "new heart" you needed for a healthier, abundant life.

❖ *Sanctus*—Imagine experiencing God's holiness—in worship or elsewhere—in a way that might inspire you to bow in reverence. How is God's transcendence (otherness) mysteriously revealed to you in God's immanence (nearness)?

❖ *Institution Narrative*—Reflect on the ways you have experienced the pattern of taking, blessing, breaking, and giving in your life. How has God taken your brokenness and transformed it into a blessing that could be given?

❖ *Memorial Acclamation*—Imagining our lives within the range of God's eternal, alpha and omega life, can you think of an event from your past that shapes your gratitude in the present and also gives you hope for the future?

❖ *Epiclesis*—Try to remember a time when you called for God's presence beside you. When have you experienced a strong sense of God's Holy Spirit beside you as an advocate, counselor, comforter, or helper—with or without the physical presence of another person?

❖ *Amen*—How do you affirm the truth and goodness of the Holy Eucharist by expressing your Amen, not just in word but also in deed after you leave the church?

❖ Do This in Remembrance—Think of how "doing this" in remembrance has helped you to better remember Christ in your life. How has Holy Eucharist enabled you to become better re-membered with a community that stands with you in times of trial?

Chapter 14

The Lord's Prayer

Draw Near with Persistence

One of Jesus' disciples said to him, "Lord, teach us to pray."

—Luke 11:1

In the Gospel according to Saint Luke, Jesus calls his followers over and over to draw near. On his journey from Galilee to Jerusalem he invites one person after another to draw near and follow him. He commends the Good Samaritan for drawing near to his neighbor and acting with God's compassion and mercy. Jesus praises Mary for drawing near to spend quality time with him, while Martha struggles with worry and the distraction of busyness.[xv]

Saint Luke also records how Jesus practices what he preaches—drawing near to his heavenly Father in prayer. And then Jesus' disciples finally ask him to show them how to draw near to God. "Lord, teach us to pray!" they ask (Luke 11:1). Those of us who follow Jesus still ask this same question, don't we? *Lord, teach us to pray! Give us the right words to say. Show us how to draw near to God!*

And now, as our Savior Christ has taught us, we are bold to say,

People and Celebrant

Our Father, who art in heaven,
    hallowed be thy Name,
    thy kingdom come,
    thy will be done,
        on earth as it is in heaven.
Give us this day our daily bread.
And forgive us our trespasses,
    as we forgive those
        who trespass against us.
And lead us not into temptation,
    but deliver us from evil.
For thine is the kingdom,
    and the power, and the glory,
    for ever and ever. Amen.

—The service for Holy Communion continues on page 364 of *The Book of Common Prayer.*

Jesus could give his disciples any of the words from the Jewish "book of common prayer," otherwise known as the Psalms.

Instead, he gives them something new. We call it the Lord's Prayer.

> "Father, hallowed be your name. Your kingdom come.
> Give us each day our daily bread. And forgive us our
> sins, for we ourselves forgive everyone indebted to us.
> And do not bring us to the time of trial."
>
> —Luke 11:2-4

The Lord's Prayer is an expression of our desire to draw near to God and our desire for God to draw near to us. Notice where this prayer is offered[xvi] during Holy Communion—right before we draw near to God's table to be fed and sustained with Christ's presence in the sacrament of bread and wine. Since about 400 years after the birth of Christ, this prayer has been a devotion intended to prepare people to receive the sacrament. Indeed, the earliest Christians identified the "daily bread" petition in the Lord's Prayer with the bread of eucharist.

If you want to witness a miracle, draw near to someone who is approaching their last breath and begin praying the Lord's Prayer. People who have followed Jesus throughout their life—even if they lack the strength to open their eyes, squeeze your hand, or say a word—often join in praying the Lord's Prayer or at least moving their lips to its cadence: "Our Father, who art in heaven, hallowed be thy name…"

Prayer is how we draw nearer to God and express our desire for God to draw near to us. When we can't figure out what to say in our prayers, we can use these words that Jesus taught us. When parents want to teach their children to pray but can't decide how to begin, they can show up at their bedside and use these words that Jesus taught us. When adult children are caring for a sick or dying parent but can't figure out what to pray, they can draw near to their bedside and use these words that Jesus taught us.

Jesus has given us words to express our heart's desire to draw near to our Father in heaven. They are not magic words. They don't cast a spell. They help us express our desire for God and God's desire for us.

We express this desire with all the forms of prayer condensed into one. We first express our desire with adoration and praise (hallowed be your name), then with intercession for all (your will be done on earth as in heaven), with petition for ourselves (give us today our daily bread), with the confession we need to make (forgive us), and with the oblation we need to give (as we forgive). Only Jesus could craft the perfect prayer.

But of course, Jesus gives us more than just words. He also coaches his disciples (and that includes us!) to be persistent in prayer. It is easy to become men and women—even priests— on a mission and miss the opportunity to draw near (like the Good Samaritan) and help God's kingdom come and God's will be done on earth as in heaven. It is easy to become busy and distracted like Martha, working to put food on the table, and miss the opportunity to draw near (like Mary) and trust God to give us this day our daily bread. It is easy to make excuses for why it's not a good time to follow Jesus and miss an opportunity to draw near and trust that God will deliver us from evil, even on the dangerous, difficult, or lonely paths we sometimes travel.

†

I once walked one of these difficult paths through the Annapurna Range of the Himalayan Mountains. For several days I trekked alone, up and down thousands of stepping stones that had been laid by hand across those mountains for generations. I learned about this trail from a stranger I met in India the month before. I don't remember his name, but he looked like Jesus (or at least how I envision Jesus—you know what I mean—olive skin, handsome face, long flowing hair, and a full beard.)

The man described an amazing journey on this mountain range and urged me to give it a try. Just like Jesus encouraged his followers about prayer, this man described an amazing experience of nearness to God and exhorted me to be persistent in pursuing it: "Search, and you will find."

The man pointed his finger at a tattered map and traced a path by which I could move from one village to the next, arriving each night at a safe place to sleep before sundown. I expressed my doubts and uncertainty about finding safe food and lodging. Like Jesus coaching his disciples about prayer, he encouraged me to try: "Ask, and it will be given you."

"There's one exception," he pointed out. "There's a place called Poon Hill, and it's a little more than a day's walk, but it is oh so worth it. So, wake up early and hit the trail out of Ulleri village. Pick up your pace and keep walking. Be persistent!"

He ignored my sigh of resignation and kept talking. "There will be a sign on the pathway. Trust it. Follow it. And climb the hill. At the top of the hill is a small house. The family is really nice. They welcome hikers who need a hot meal and a warm place to sleep." Like Jesus urging those of us who want to believe the promise, he said, "Knock, and the door will be opened for you."

Do you have mixed feelings about drawing near to God? You're in good company since most of the people in the Bible experienced these same feelings. Do you have doubts about whether you can walk this path alone? You're in good company: The church is filled with people who choose to walk together on this journey of faith.

Do you find it hard to be persistent in prayer when your health keeps declining, when you can't find a job, or when death claims a loved one? Do you find that you have done everything in your power to solve a problem, mend a relationship, or help a friend or family member, and there is nothing else you can do but ask God to intervene?

Jesus urges those of us who follow him to be persistent in our prayer: "Ask, and it will be given to you; search, and you will find; knock, and the door will be opened for you" (Luke 11:9).

The day I walked toward Poon Hill was cloudy and foggy. I could see anywhere from five steps to 100 yards in front of me, but the mountains were completely hidden from view. I tried to keep a quick, steady pace throughout the day, but because of the thick clouds, darkness was falling when I finally found the promised sign.

I knew I could turn back toward Ghorepani village and find a guest house without much effort or worry. What I did not know was how long it would take to press on and climb the last, snow-covered hill. All I could remember was the voice of the stranger who reminded me of Jesus: "Be persistent. Search and you will find."

So I climbed into the darkness—exhausted, cold, and afraid. Eventually, just as promised, a solitary shack stood at the top of Poon Hill. I could see the warm glow of a fire piercing tiny gaps between the boards of the door. A few sparks rose out of the makeshift chimney.

I knocked, and the door opened. An old man answered with a smile as if he had been waiting for my arrival all day. "Namaste," he greeted with a bow. "Namaste," I replied with tears in my eyes.

He pointed to a place where I could spread out my sleeping bag and then handed me a plate of hot food, including—and I am not making this up—a slice of freshly baked apple pie. Like the Good Samaritan, he was a compassionate and merciful neighbor to me. He was, literally, a perfect stranger.

The next morning, the light of dawn pierced through the boards of the wall near my face. Even from the tiny sliver of light, I could see it was a clear morning. I pulled on my boots, threw a blanket around my shoulders and ran outside to discover that I was surrounded by peaks rising upwards of 26,000 feet—a crystal clear, jagged horizon.

Just below the top of the hill on which I was standing was a soft bed of clouds pushed by strong winds in a swirling pattern. It was as if I stood upon the still point—the axis—a thin place where heaven and earth meet. With the help of perfect strangers, I discovered a joyful place to draw near to God and give thanks.

Jesus is calling us to draw near and trust. Fear not. Be persistent. Our Father in heaven will bring us, with all the saints, into the joy of the eternal kingdom. And this is precisely what we ask through Jesus Christ—by him, and with him, and in him—when we pray with the words he taught us.

These are not magic words, but they are sacred words. Moreover, they are sturdy enough to last us a lifetime. Our Lord's Prayer enables us, even with our dying breath, to express the most basic and important things we need to say to our Father in heaven. This prayer helps us to draw near to the kingdom, and the power, and the glory, for ever and ever. Amen.

Reflecting on Our Story with God

❖ When have perfect strangers encouraged or helped you discover the joy of God's beauty, goodness, or truth?

❖ Think of a time you were persistent. In what ways were you challenged? In what ways were you blessed?

❖ When have you been a perfect stranger by drawing near to someone in need?

Celebrating Our Story with God

❖ If possible, plan a safe but challenging journey that stretches your familiar comfort zone. If this is not physically or financially possible, then journey vicariously through other peoples' stories or pictures.

❖ With a little persistence, any of us can draw near to God and to our neighbors—even those we have never met. Whether you bake apple pies or express your love through other gifts, find a new (or old) neighbor to bless.

Chapter 15

Christ Our Passover Is Sacrificed for Us

Lifeline

Jesus said, "Go and learn what this means, 'I desire mercy, and not sacrifice.'"

—Matthew 9:13

Immediately following the Lord's Prayer, the priest lifts the consecrated (blessed) bread and breaks it. This follows the pattern of Jesus at the feeding of the five thousand, at the Last Supper with his disciples, and at the first supper in Emmaus. He takes...blesses...and breaks before he gives.

This moment in the Holy Eucharist is sometimes called "the fraction" to signal that something that was originally whole

The Breaking of the Bread

The Celebrant breaks the consecrated Bread.

A period of silence is kept.

Then may be sung or said

[Alleluia.] Christ our Passover is sacrificed for us;
Therefore let us keep the feast. [*Alleluia.*]

—The service for Holy Communion continues
on page 364 of *The Book of Common Prayer.*

and perfect was broken for our benefit. The fraction of the bread is our visual and audible reminder of sacrifice. At the fraction, we recognize that brokenness is part of the human condition, even for Jesus Christ whose body was broken and buried. We honor the sacrifice Jesus was willing to endure for the sake of love. We remember that God's love involved real sacrifice for us, as does our practice of love for others in God's name.

This moment is so important that *The Book of Common Prayer* instructs the priest and people to keep silent for a moment before continuing. This quiet reverence marks a pause in our celebration before we continue with a spoken or sung anthem. After this moment of silence, the most common response to the fraction is a simple statement between the priest and people. With the exception of the penitential season of Lent, we add the celebratory word "Alleluia!" to indicate our joy for all that Christ has done for us.

In order to explore a little more deeply what it means for Christ to be our Passover sacrifice and feast, we need to look at the Gospel according to Saint John.

In John's Gospel, Jesus first appears on the scene as a rabbi (teacher), inviting his disciples (students) to "come and see." A few days later, they end up in Cana of Galilee where Jesus performs the most winsome miracle you can imagine. He helps out some poor chap whose daughter's special wedding day is quickly turning into a disaster as the wine being served at the reception runs out.

The question is: Who wouldn't be interested in serving as this man's disciple? Hanging out at wedding feasts, enjoying fine wine, socializing with happy people. Sounds like fun!

After this, John writes that Jesus went to Capernaum for a few days with his family and these new disciples. Capernaum was a small town on the north shore of the Sea of Galilee. Translation: fresh fish, uncrowded beaches, spring break!

Then it is time for another big party, the feast of the Passover![xvii] On this one night a year, all the people of Israel, wherever they are, drop everything to remember and celebrate how God delivered them out of Egyptian slavery. They celebrate with roasted lamb, olives, dates, herbs, unleavened bread, fine wine, music, and dancing. You can guess the location of the grandest celebration of Passover—Jerusalem. You can also guess what Jesus and his new friends do. They make a road trip! I can imagine one disciple whispering to another as they travel up to Jerusalem, remembering how much they enjoyed the wedding feast in Cana and the several days in Capernaum, "We ain't seen nothin' yet." And boy, were they ever right.

They enter the temple compound, with throngs of people everywhere, and—to use a contemporary phrase—Jesus begins to "freak out." Right there on the spot he makes a whip of cords and begins to use it. He whips animals that belong to other people. He dumps out money that belongs to other people. He yells at people who think they are minding their own business.

Just imagine the uncomfortable looks those brand-new disciples must have exchanged with one another that afternoon in the courtyard. They must have been dumbfounded. Jesus goes from being the hero of the wedding feast in Galilee to the spoiler at the Passover Feast in Jerusalem. We can imagine the disciples asking themselves, "Wait a minute. Is this what I signed up for?" I suspect we sometimes ask ourselves the same question.

What do we do when our comfortable image of Jesus gets disturbed?

Near the beginning of his book, *The Jesus I Never Knew,* Philip Yancey writes about the Jesus he thought he knew: "Someone kind and reassuring, with no sharp edges at all—a Mister Rogers before the age of children's television."[xviii] He imagined Jesus as a good shepherd, someone who encouraged people to be nice to one another.

Then Yancey asks the very demanding question. "How would telling people to be nice to one another get a man crucified? What government would execute Mister Rogers or Captain Kangaroo?"[xix]

The answer is simple and obvious. Being nice does not get you crucified. Governments don't execute nice people. They execute people they believe to be dangerous and threatening.

We need to remember that Jesus is not passionate about being nice. He is passionate about his Father's house. The Gospel according to Saint John records Jesus' words this way: "Zeal for your house will consume me!"xx

Jesus understands the true purpose of the temple—to make God's presence available on earth. And Jesus is filled with zeal about sharing God's presence with everyone. Not surprisingly, Jesus is filled with anger toward those who barricade God's presence behind their own greed or dishonesty.

One of the important lessons in holy scripture is that anger is not the opposite of love—indifference is. God may be angry out of love, but God is never indifferent.

The very feast that Jesus and his disciples go to Jerusalem to celebrate—the Passover—is the crowning example of God's loving anger over the Hebrew's enslavement by the Egyptian Pharaoh. God was not indifferent to the plight of Moses and the Hebrews. The Lord forcibly delivered them out of slavery in Egypt.

The story of Exodus is echoed in the first of the Ten Commandments: "I am the Lord your God, who brought you out of the land of Egypt, out of the house of slavery; you shall have no other gods before me."

Re-read this commandment and try to think about it in a new light, not so much as rule number one but as a loving declaration of good news about freedom, with God essentially offering a lifeline, *I have brought you freedom; nothing and nobody will come between us any longer!*

†

The day after I arrived in New Delhi, India, I stumbled out of bed with one of those aching, sweating, chilling fevers that make you feel not only sick but also homesick. Still, I needed to register with the U.S. Embassy.

It had been several weeks since I had called home. This was before the days of prepaid calling cards and cell phones. In the places I had been traveling, I had to stand in long lines for hours at specially designated switchboards and pay expensive fees (and bribes) for the privilege of placing a short, international call.

I was walking down a side street in New Delhi when I noticed a church. In a predominantly Hindu region, the church stuck out and so did the man standing in the front. After showing me the church, he invited me to his home next door for a soft drink.

Normally, I would have rejected the invitation. Drugging vulnerable travelers in order to steal passports and money is an ever-present risk for a solo traveler. The man seemed decent, though perhaps I let my guard down because I didn't feel well. Maybe he could see how pathetic I looked and was the next Good Samaritan on my pathway.

Nervously, I entered his small home next to the church. He brought me a cola from a little refrigerator and invited me to sit down. Then he asked me two questions: "When is the last time you spoke with your mother?" (Several weeks.) "And what is her phone number?" He picked up his black telephone, dialed it, handed me the receiver with a smile, and said, "Talk as long as you want."

My new friend had an international watts line as part of his export business. Like Christ, he was zealous about eliminating the barrier to a loving relationship. Like Christ, he was zealous about offering a direct connection—a lifeline—to my house and with my loving parent.

Now, let's return to that spectacle two thousand years ago in the courtyard of the temple in Jerusalem. Why is Jesus so angry when everyone else is in a great mood celebrating the Feast of Passover?

I believe it is as simple as this: I think the money changers and profiteers in the temple courtyard remind Jesus of Pharaoh by inserting themselves between God and God's people. Like Pharaoh, they have to be forcibly pushed aside. The people's relationship with God needs to be restored. Nothing and nobody should stand in the way—not religious leaders, religious tradition, or even religious law!

Jesus is consumed with zeal about allowing the divine relationship to grow and deepen for all people. At the wedding feast, he removes a distraction so there might be a full celebration of communion. At the Passover Feast, he removes a barrier so there might be a full celebration of communion.

In fact, Jesus becomes so consumed with zeal about this relationship between God and humanity that instead of *celebrating* the Passover Feast, he *becomes* the Passover Feast.

"Christ, our Passover, is sacrificed for us!" the priest proclaims as part of the eucharistic prayer. No more cattle or sheep or doves are required. No more greedy power brokers stand in the way. No more slavery—to work or money or any other idol we might make or have put upon us by someone else. No more fear. And no more indifference to the needs of others. Christ acts decisively to put an end to all that madness once and for all.

All of Christ's zeal, all of the divine affection, and all of the Father's devotion is available for us to receive and share with a hungry world. In other words, "Alleluia! Christ our Passover is sacrificed for us. Therefore, let us keep the feast. Alleluia!"

Reflecting on Our Story with God

❖ Where is the focus of your passion?

❖ Do you have any anger about injustice that you feel a need to express?

❖ What would you be willing to create a public spectacle about?

❖ When have you had to make sacrifices for the sake of love?

Celebrating Our Story with God

❖ Consider how honoring our baptismal promise to strive for justice and peace might require us to disrupt systems or people who stand between the grace, freedom, and peace that God intends to have as a direct lifeline with all people.

❖ Consider how honoring our baptismal promise to repent might require us to get out of the way when we find ourselves standing like a barrier between those who seek mercy and our loving God who wants to give it.

Chapter 16

The Body of Christ, the Bread of Heaven

Taste and See

Taste and see that the Lord is good; happy are they who trust in him!
—Psalm 34:8

Theologians and people in the pew have debated since at least the Middle Ages about what happens to the blessed sacrament during Holy Communion. Do the bread and wine turn into Christ's body and blood—a process the church calls transubstantiation? What does it mean for the substance of something to change? Can it be measured, analyzed, or proven? Should it be?

In the Episcopal Church we subscribe to the view that the real presence of Christ is manifest in the Sacrament of Holy Communion. In classic Anglican fashion, we don't attempt to

Facing the people, the Celebrant says the following Invitation

The Gifts of God for the People of God.

and may add   Take them in remembrance that Christ
died for you,
and feed on him in your hearts by faith,
with thanksgiving.

*The ministers receive the Sacrament in both kinds, and then immediately
deliver it to the people.*

The Bread and the Cup are given to the communicants with these words

The Body (Blood) of our Lord Jesus Christ keep you in
everlasting life. [*Amen.*]

or with these words

The Body of Christ, the bread of heaven. [*Amen.*]
The Blood of Christ, the cup of salvation. [*Amen.*]

*During the ministration of Communion, hymns, psalms, or anthems may
be sung.*

—The service for Holy Communion continues
on page 364 of *The Book of Common Prayer.*

define that idea too explicitly. We leave room for each person
to discern how God in Christ is truly present in the sacrament.

A lover who attempts to measure, analyze, and prove how
much love is present in red roses will inevitably fail—as words
do—to explain what is real and true. The foolish lover who

tries to explain the species and type of the genus rosa in the bouquet will only get stuck on the thorns. The wise lover lets the roses speak for themselves. The wise lover who trusts that the love is real and true will also be evident to the beloved.

We can be curious about what happens to the elements of Holy Communion and even debate the variety of ideas the wider church has held about this question across the centuries. As with many of the church's ideas, I believe there is more than one faithful way to discern how God is real and present in the sacrament.

But I am persuaded that God is far more interested in what happens to his children during the eucharist. I believe God is more interested in the change that takes place within us.

A sacrament is an outward and visible sign of an inward and spiritual grace. So while it is important to think about and honor the outward and visible signs we celebrate in our story with God, it is even more essential that we focus upon and give thanks for the inward and spiritual grace we receive at this sacred gathering.

Part of the inward and spiritual grace we receive through eucharist is discovering a whole new way of believing. At Jesus' transfiguration on the mountaintop, Peter, James, and John discover that "seeing is believing." In Saint Paul's letter to the Romans, he claims that "hearing leads to believing" (10:7). Yet, the oldest, most traditional source of belief according to Moses, the psalmist, and Jesus himself is that "*tasting* is believing."

Moses talks about not living by bread alone and yet describes the promised land as a place where the Israelites will eat bread without scarcity. The psalmist proclaims, "Taste and see that the Lord is good" (34:8). And Jesus talks about bread from heaven, bread of life, and bread as his very own flesh! Bread conveys a lot of symbolic information in Holy Scripture, and much of it is hard to understand.

Remember the story from Saint Mark's Gospel when Jesus rescues the disciples—again—from a stormy night at sea? As Jesus climbs into the boat and we are ready to cheer for this remarkable save, Mark records that the disciples were astounded, for they did not understand about the loaves (presumably from the feeding of the five thousand they had just completed).[xxi]

Not only did they not understand but Mark also reports that their hearts were hardened. A literal translation of the Greek describes their hearts as calloused. Calloused hearts? We're talking about fishermen here. We might understand calloused hands, but how is it that Jesus' friends have calloused hearts— over bread, no less?

I believe we know more about calloused hearts than we care to admit. The callouses are not a result of God's transcendence safely beyond the clouds, well out of reach. No—you only get callouses when you get rubbed the wrong way. And you cannot get rubbed the wrong way unless you're close to the source of discomfort.

Consider what happens to Moses when he draws near to God on Mount Sinai. He is burned so badly that he has to wear a veil in public. Here is a guy God calls out of Midian, where he is leading a fairly anonymous life as an Egyptian fugitive. God sends him back to Egypt and pits him against the most powerful ruler on earth. God then saddles him with leading people who complain all the time. In spite of all this (or perhaps because of it), Moses says to the Israelites, "One does not live by bread alone, but by every word that comes forth from the mouth of the Lord" (Deuteronomy 8:3).

After forty years of manna in the wilderness, we can rest assured that Moses knows what he is talking about. He knows God, he knows about God's bread, and he knows about God's Word. He doesn't know this because of God's transcendence somewhere safely above the clouds. He knows this because the cloud of God came down and led them out of bondage in Egypt. He knows this because God rains down manna upon them to eat.

And what does Moses say to his people? "You shall eat your fill and bless the Lord your God for the good land he has given you" (Deuteronomy 8:10). Moses has every reason to have a calloused heart, but in his faithfulness, he calls upon the people to eat their fill and bless the Lord. Moses understands that tasting is believing.

Saint Paul could rub people the wrong way. In the midst of his letter to the Ephesians, Paul gives a list of instructions about how they should get along, even when they feel callused. [xxii] Paul's list is summarized in the offertory sentence that invites us forward at Holy Communion to receive the Body of Christ, the bread of heaven. "Walk in love, as Christ loved us and gave himself up for us, an offering and sacrifice to God." [xxiii] Like Moses, Paul understands that tasting is believing.

Let's look more closely at what Jesus says. After all, he is the one who takes this powerful metaphor of "bread" and applies it to himself.

First, Jesus repeatedly uses "I AM," the sacred name of God that was considered in his day to be too holy to be spoken. Then, Jesus says he will raise people up on the last day. Imagine being a contemporary of Jesus and hearing him or anyone make such an inconceivable claim.

If that is not enough to shock and stun people, Jesus tells them that the bread he will give for the life of the world is his flesh. This statement is not only a scandalous affront to Jewish dietary laws, but it also flouts the timeless and universal prohibition against the repulsive act of eating human flesh. If we listen closely to what Jesus is saying, his words will probably rub us the wrong way and give us callouses.

Jesus is clear that he is not just an imitator of God by doing God's will. Rather, he is God, and he is uncomfortably close. We can see him, hear him, touch and smell him, and now—we learn—we can even taste him.

The Real Presence of Christ is not just a matter of past tense, as if Jesus' gift of love only had relevance two thousand years ago. Nor is this offering only a matter of future tense, as if Jesus' gift of life pertains only to a future, heavenly realm. Jesus does not say "whoever believes *will have* eternal life."[xxiv] He says, "whoever believes is *having* eternal life."

We need to remember that in the world-famous verse—John 3:16—Jesus is speaking in the present, continuous tense. Jesus does not show us that tasting *was* believing or that tasting *will be* believing. Jesus has shown us that tasting is *believing*—in the present.

The Real Presence of Christ is here and now. We are still knowing Christ—presently and continuously—in the breaking of the bread and in the receiving of the bread. Furthermore, we receive the gift of Christ even when, perhaps especially when, we have failed to share love as Christ has loved us.

The sacrament of Holy Communion is essential for us. Only when we commune with God can we loosen our hearts and hands from the struggles that make them tough and calloused and align ourselves with Christ. Only when we commune with God can we walk in love as Christ loved us and gave himself for us.

The true miracle of the Holy Eucharist is that Christ welcomes us and urges us to eat our fill, hoping not only that we will "get it" but also that we will share it with other hungry bodies and souls. We bless the Lord when we taste, believe, and share the love of God.

This may sound like a weighty burden. If it does, and if this chapter is rubbing you the wrong way, then you have missed the essential point of the gospel. While we partake of the bread and wine, the sacrament of Holy Communion is not primarily about us. It is about God. The teachings of Moses, the psalmist, Paul, and Jesus are not about those who receive the bread. The point of all these passages is about the One who gives the bread. The fact that Jesus is willing to share his bread—and ultimately his life—with his friends and with his enemies illustrates how powerfully God's glory is revealed in Jesus Christ.

And this revelation of glory is essentially a revelation of love. Love means looking into the faces of your friends and even your enemies and sharing a bit of yourself with them. Moses, Paul, and Jesus teach us how to live faithfully, by "walking in love as Christ first loved us," and by giving ourselves to one another "as Christ gave himself up for us."

We have a template for this faithful living and faithful giving in the sacrament of Holy Communion. Every time we come forward to taste and believe, we are given the profound offering of God's love through Christ's body and blood. "The Body of Christ, given for thee! The Blood of Christ, shed for thee!"

Christ invites us out of generosity and beckons us toward generosity. In other words, we receive the invitation to Christ's table because God is generous. By accepting that invitation, we are enabled to participate in this same, generous aspect of divine life.

Being generous means keeping the feast—not keeping it as in keeping it for ourselves but as in *keeping it going*. We keep the feast going by sharing the love of Christ. We share the love of Christ with those who gather beside us at the table—rejoicing with those who rejoice, weeping with those who weep, forgiving and being forgiven with those who walk in love as Christ loves us.

We also keep the feast going by taking the love of Christ into the world and sharing with those who are not at the table. In our modern consumer culture, we are generally quite good at "eating our fill," but we are woefully inadequate at "blessing the Lord by sharing God's abundance with others."

Roman Catholic Archbishop Hélder Câmara served some of the poorest areas of Brazil from 1964 to 1985. Listen to what he said about bread: "When I give food to the poor, they call me a saint. When I ask why the poor have no food, they call me a communist." Sounds like Archbishop Câmara rubbed some people the wrong way—and gave them callouses. He also sounds a lot like Jesus, who invites all to the banquet table.

We make manifest the heavenly feast when we keep it going, both by feeding the poor and by asking why the poor have no food. We keep the feast going by praying, working, and giving abundantly to spread God's loving kingdom on earth as in heaven.

Tasting, believing, and sharing is not a burden. It is how our calloused hearts regain sensitivity to God's mysterious and miraculous work around us and within us. It is how we say thank you to God.

Just as Moses taught the Israelites, the sacrament of Holy Communion reminds us that tasting is believing. So, "You shall eat your fill and then bless the Lord for everything[xxv] he has given you."

Reflecting on Our Story with God

❖ Think of a time when a teacher or a friend "rubbed you the wrong way" but later you came to a new or different understanding of how their words or deeds were actually compassionate.

❖ Reflect on the callused parts of your heart that may have lost an important sensitivity to how the love and mercy of God is at work in the world around us and within us.

Celebrating Our Story with God

❖ Consider a way in which you might not only feed the poor but also be an advocate by asking hard questions about the reasons the poor have no food.

❖ The next time you receive Holy Communion, consider the fullness of how you have seen our Lord in the gathered assembly, heard our Lord through the lessons and prayers, and tasted our Lord in the sacrament of bread and wine. Having "tasted and seen," how will you now share his real, loving presence in outward and visible ways in the world?

Chapter 17

Post-Communion Thanksgiving

Glorify in Living Color

O men and women everywhere, glorify the Lord, praise him and highly exalt him for ever.

—Canticle 12, A Song of Creation
The Book of Common Prayer

Imagine you have just finished dinner at the home of someone you love. Maybe it is a family member or a close friend, perhaps even someone in whom you have a romantic interest. The meal was perfect. The dishes have been cleared, and it is almost time to go. You want to find just the right words to say, "thank you." You want the other person to know just how grateful you are.

This is the natural logic of the post-communion thanksgiving prayer. After all is said and done, we simply want to offer one final "thank you" for the love of God we experienced by being

After Communion, the Celebrant says

Let us pray.

Celebrant and People

Eternal God, heavenly Father,
you have graciously accepted us as living members
of your Son our Savior Jesus Christ,
and you have fed us with spiritual food
in the Sacrament of his Body and Blood.
Send us now into the world in peace,
and grant us strength and courage
to love and serve you
with gladness and singleness of heart;
through Christ our Lord. Amen.

or the following

Almighty and everliving God,
we thank you for feeding us with the spiritual food
of the most precious Body and Blood
of your Son our Savior Jesus Christ;
and for assuring us in these holy mysteries
that we are living members of the Body of your Son,
and heirs of your eternal kingdom.
And now, Father, send us out
to do the work you have given us to do,
to love and serve you
as faithful witnesses of Christ our Lord.
To him, to you, and to the Holy Spirit,
be honor and glory, now and for ever. Amen.

—The service for Holy Communion continues
on page 365 of *The Book of Common Prayer.*

forgiven, healed, and renewed. One way we give thanks in that moment is to pray for the strength and courage to continue showing our gratitude as members of Christ's Body after we leave.

One of the post-communion prayers thanks our heavenly Father "for assuring us in these holy mysteries that we *are* living members of the Body of your Son our Savior Jesus Christ…"[xxvi] In other words, the holy mysteries of God's love are not confined to the ancient past; they are alive with us and within us in the present. The title of this book attempts to convey the lively presence of God's love that we encounter through the gifts of communion. Indeed, we, the people of God, celebrate receiving the gifts of God.

Another post-communion prayer asks God for "strength and courage to love and serve…"[xxvii] as we take our thanksgiving (our *eucharisteo*) out in the world. We practice thanksgiving not only with our lips but also in our lives since gratitude is most clearly expressed by word *and* example. One of the important, enduring ways we express our gratitude to our Father in heaven is to love and care for all of God's children. If you want to know how pleasing this is, ask any parent who has been blessed to witness one child caring for another sibling!

All that we say and do as an expression of gratitude glorifies God. One of the important things that Jesus taught—by word and example—is that religion does not glorify God, following rules does not glorify God, and calling down or calling out other people does not glorify God. The action that most clearly and effectively glorifies God is loving one's neighbor as oneself.

The Gospel according to Saint John reinforces this message. Near the end of his life, Jesus prays to God with thanksgiving for the opportunity to glorify the Father and for the chance to be glorified as the Father's true and only Son. This prayer is commonly referred to as the "high priestly prayer."

> Jesus looked up to heaven and said, "Father, the hour has come; glorify your Son so that the Son may glorify you, since you have given him authority over all people, to give eternal life to all whom you have given him. And this is eternal life, that they may know you, the only true God, and Jesus Christ whom you have sent. I glorified you on earth by finishing the work that you gave me to do. So now, Father, glorify me in your own presence with the glory that I had in your presence before the world existed."
>
> —John 17:1b-5

It is a beautiful and powerful prayer. But if you're not a high priest (and none of us are), this high priestly prayer sounds so exalted and spiritual that it can be tough to figure out what it means. After the fourth reference to glorification our minds may wander, or at least wonder what Jesus is talking about.

This prayer can sound so distant and so strange. If we are asked to say the blessing at a meal, most of us do not use words like glorification. We have a hard time relating to a word like that.

Jesus' prayer about glorification is called a high priestly prayer, but it begins as a prayer about his oneness with the Father, with his communion with our Father in heaven. Jesus expresses his thanksgiving for this perfect communion, which enabled an earthly ministry glorifying God and blessing God's other children. Jesus is the pioneer of a gratitude-based faith that glorifies God by loving and serving other people. And then he prays, "Father, I glorified you on earth by finishing the work that you gave me to do." Jesus is the faithful presence of God in human form, loving and serving others—not only neighbors and friends but also foreigners and enemies.

This prayer also makes evident that the hour was coming when Jesus would have to say goodbye to his closest friends and followers. And Jesus knew it. So, when he prayed this prayer, he was offering the words to say "thank you" and then asking for strength and courage for his dear friends after he was gone.

If you took the time to write down a final, goodbye prayer for your friends, what would you pray? Would you talk about how you have been honored (dare we say "glorified") to be their friend? This is what Jesus is saying. Would you pray that they too might be honored ("glorified") to claim the relationship they have with you? This is what Jesus is praying.

Faithfulness is all about relationship—relationship with God and with one another as members of Christ's Body. When we are in a healthy relationship with God and one another, then we become the faithful presence of God in human form, loving and serving others. In this way, we glorify God.

†

I once attended a middle school graduation ceremony in a basketball gymnasium. As with most graduation ceremonies, it ran a little long. My mind began to wander off in the midst of the seemingly endless awards and recognitions.

Well into the ceremony, a boy's name was called, and the usual polite applause followed from students, teachers, and family members. I was fidgeting to get comfortable. Other people were checking their camera batteries and sending text messages, conspicuous signs of their boredom.

However, as this young boy came forward, it became apparent that he was a special education student. The polite applause did not fade as quickly as with all the other names that had been called. Instead, the applause was sustained as he made his way to the front of the gym.

The boy's mother was sitting directly across the gym from me, near the podium. There was no question she was the mother because she was positively radiant with glory and honor as he looked up at her. She jumped to her feet when he passed by on his way to receive the award from the principal, and the applause throughout the gym grew louder. He was looking up and smiling, basking in the glory of that moment.

He received his award and turned back to face the student body, and the mother simply could not contain herself. Jumping up and down and clapping could not fully express the love she had, and so she came bouncing down the bleachers and ran out onto the gym floor and gave her son the biggest hug you can imagine—right there in front of God and everybody! The gym simply went wild. We were cheering with delight at the chance to see so much love and so much glory and honor, right there in front of us.

This is a perfect visualization of the high priestly prayer, being fleshed out by a mother and a son: the son being glorified by his mother, the mother being glorified by the son.

Eternal life was depicted in that moment when the boredom, distractions, and fidgeting of chronological time vanished because love could not be contained between the two of them. The love that poured out between a mother and her son was so true, so good, and so beautiful that it claimed everyone's full attention. The glory of that relationship was a delight to behold.

This is Jesus' prayer for his disciples, including us. Jesus prays that we might be one, as he and the Father are one, embracing one another in relationships of love that overflow and glorify God.

Jesus' prayer for us is that we might behold all that is true, good, and beautiful in the Divine Life of his perfect relationship with the Father and the Spirit. Jesus prays that this glory might shine on us and inspire not only our praise for God but also our love for others.

This is what we are trying to articulate in the post-communion thanksgiving. One last time before we leave the worship service, we try to find the right words to glorify and exalt our Father in heaven in the way of his true and only Son. We use this final thanksgiving prayer to celebrate our story with God. It may not be a high priestly prayer, but it still expresses our desire to glorify God, always and everywhere.

Like the love shared between that mother and son, the love we experience in Holy Communion simply cannot be contained between God and us. These holy mysteries shine with such glory and honor because God's love is overflowing. So we look to Jesus, the pioneer, who has shown us how to pour out this glory in a gratitude-based faith that blesses all of God's children.

Reflecting on Our Story with God

❖ Reflect on the ways you glorify God with all that you have and all that you are. Perhaps this is a love directed at a beloved family member or friend, one that overflows in ways others might witness.

❖ Try to remember a time when you witnessed a love so true, good, and beautiful between others that you experienced the joy of simply beholding it for yourself.

Celebrating Our Story with God

❖ Try writing your own, regular thanksgiving prayer. Perhaps you may pray it after dinner or before you go to sleep.

❖ Write your own final goodbye prayer to place with your permanent documents. What will you say? How will you describe the ways you have been honored (glorified) to be connected with those who might see the letter one day? How will you pray that they, too, might be honored (glorified) in the future to claim the relationship they had with you?

Chapter 18

The Dismissal

Taking the Training Wheels Off

Jesus said, "Remember, I am with you always, to the end of the age."
—Matthew 28:20

At the end of the Holy Eucharist, we are all about to become apostles. The word "apostle" is derived from the Greek, *apostolos*, which means one who is sent. Just as we gather in God's name at the beginning of Holy Eucharist, so also are we sent out in God's name at the end.

God's loving name is both the centripetal force that gathers up and the centrifugal force that disperses out. This is the signature of a faithful life—adoring (worshiping) what is true, good, and beautiful at our center, while at the same time being in relationship with all of life that emanates from this Source. Just as breathing requires inhalation and exhalation, God's Spirit both draws us in and sends us out.

During Holy Communion, we sing, speak, and hear God's story before affirming it as our own. We offer our prayers, our peace, and our power before receiving them all back as gifts

The Bishop when present, or the Priest, may bless the people.

The Deacon, or the Celebrant, dismisses them with these words

> Let us go forth in the name of Christ.

People   Thanks be to God.

or this

Deacon   Go in peace to love and serve the Lord.

People   Thanks be to God.

or this

Deacon   Let us go forth into the world,
                 rejoicing in the power of the Spirit.

People   Thanks be to God.

or this

Deacon   Let us bless the Lord.

People   Thanks be to God.

From the Easter Vigil through the Day of Pentecost "Alleluia, alleluia" may be added to any of the dismissals.

The People respond   Thanks be to God. Alleluia, alleluia.

—The service for Holy Communion concludes
on page 366 of *The Book of Common Prayer*.

of forgiveness, healing, and renewal. Back and forth, drawn in and sent out: This is the reciprocal nature of relationship that we celebrate in Holy Communion. In the simplest of terms, we are being fed by God's love in order to be sent out for thanks*giving*.

By all counts we should be ready for this moment when it is time to leave and return to the world. Yet, I am always deeply mindful of just how hard it is for many people to take that next step.

Each and every Sunday, I suspect many of us feel reluctant to take on the next week's bumps and bruises—figurative and literal—at work, at home, or in school. How can an hour's worth of worship prepare us for a week's worth of risk, disappointment, pain, sickness, or abuse?

It is a lot to expect, especially because we resemble those first apostles of Jesus more than we might think. Like the very first apostles, we are imperfect, confused, and unsure of ourselves. So, how does Jesus pray for his disciples when they feel this way?

As expressed in the previous chapter, our post-communion thanksgiving prayer flows naturally from the glorifying, first half of Jesus' high priestly prayer. Likewise, our final dismissal conveys the spirit of the last half of Jesus' prayer.

This is the moment when Jesus prays for his apostles precisely because of their uncertainty, confusion, doubt, and fear. He prays for their protection, knowing firsthand that this world can be an unforgiving place.

> Holy Father, protect them in your name that you have
> given me, so that they may be one, as we are one. While
> I was with them, I protected them in your name that you
> have given me. I am not asking you to take them out of
> the world, but I ask you to protect them from the evil
> one. As you have sent me into the world, so I have sent
> them into the world.
> —John 17:11b, 12a, 15, 18

I find that I have prayed some form of this prayer many times with my own children. Unfortunately, there is no manual that can definitively tell you when the time is right for your children to take new risks. There is no simple answer for when we should expose our children to new dangers or hurts. There is not a perfect time to let them move farther out into a world we know we don't control. Jesus knows this, too.

†

Some states consider fifteen years old to be the right age to issue a permit for our children to take on the risks associated with driving a motor vehicle. I have been painfully reminded of this fact each time one of my daughters reached that teeth-gnashing threshold.

I was also reminded of another day nine years earlier—just nine *short* years earlier—when I ventured out with each of my girls and a small pink bicycle, holding the wrench that would remove the training wheels from either side of the back tire.

You know the kind of Saturday I'm talking about. The one when you know it would be wise to have a wet washcloth on hand, not to mention some antibiotic anointment and band aids. You know there will be "strawberries" in her future; you just don't know if they will be on the hands, or elbows, or knees, or all three.

How are we to respond to these moments, as parents and grandparents, as mentors or teachers? While the operator's manual will tell us how to take off the training wheels, it doesn't tell us when or where. It would be nice if there were a sure-fire, easy plan for exposing those we love to new risks (and rewards) in this world, but there is not.

It is much easier to shelter and protect than to set free, let go, and even push from the safety of the nest. These challenges of faith demand the most courage and strength.

In the final half of the high priestly prayer, Jesus takes the training wheels off for his apostles and sends them into the risky, dangerous world.

To understand how unprepared they must feel, reflect back over the arc of the apostles' life with Jesus after his crucifixion. They first suffer the shock of an empty tomb. Then they endure the disbelief of hearing one another talk about seeing him again. The apostles continue harboring doubts and fears, even as they share a meal with Jesus after his resurrection. In fact, moments before Jesus' final promise, "I am with you always…", some of the disciples still doubt, according to Saint Matthew.[xxviii]

It is a very short distance from the apostles' shock and utter disbelief to this final goodbye. Seems like just when we want to shelter ourselves, Jesus informs us the training wheels are coming off. When we shrink before the demands before us, Jesus prays for us to face the risks with strength and courage.

I think I waited too long to pull out the wrench to remove the training wheels from that pink bicycle. There is never a good time to permit your child to suffer cuts and scrapes. There is never ground hard enough to make peddling easy or grass soft enough to cushion the fall. Life just does not seem fair—to child or parent.

Life may not have seemed fair to Jesus' friends either. They witness his arrest, torture, and death. They are confronted with his unbelievable resurrection. They are challenged with the risks and dangers of continuing to follow Jesus in a risky world. They are leaving the comfort of what had been safe and secure.

And Jesus is removing the training wheels. Jesus pushes his disciples every step of the way. So we should notice what Jesus does as the responsible adult in this situation. He prays.

If you re-read through the entire high priestly prayer, you might notice how often the word "give" appears. Jesus uses some version of the word "give" or "gift" nine times in only a few sentences. This is no mistake or byproduct of sloppy editing. Jesus clearly understands his disciples as a gift from God, and he entrusts these friends to his Father's care when he can no longer be physically present to protect them. Jesus prays for his disciples to be one. In other words, he prays for them to treasure the gift of sticking together when the going gets tough, just as Jesus sticks with our heavenly Father when things are tough.

Jesus gives us the gift of a prayer and an example. A gift—by definition—is something to be given. A gift is something you have to let go. Jesus gives his life that we might be able to live abundantly. Jesus lets go so we can try it for ourselves.

Love does not control; it lets go. From the beginning Christ knows of the big risks and chooses to trust anyway. From the beginning, Christ knows there will be deep hurts and chooses to love anyway.

We have enough life experience to know about the big risks and deep hurts, and yet it is still not easy to choose trust. It is not easy to choose love. It is not easy to let go.

The story of God features risky and painful choices between a Father and a Son, which love made possible and bearable.

Our story with God still unfolds with risks and hurts made bearable through love and communion with God and one another.

The training wheels lay in the grass near the sidewalk. It was time for me to let go. "Please God, don't let her fall too hard." *I know she's going to fall.* "Please don't let her forget to use the brake in the steep places." *I know she's going to pedal too fast.* "Please don't let her get hurt and feel discouraged." *I know she's going to get hurt and feel discouraged.*

Jesus prays to his Father, *I am not asking you to take them out of the world, but I ask you to protect them...* You see, Jesus knows we are going to fall. Jesus knows we will go too fast. Jesus knows we will get hurt and discouraged. Since we are not exempt from these things, he prays for us to persevere *through* these things.

I once had a phone conversation with someone who claimed not to be religious. She was caring for an ailing parent. Maybe she was caring for the person who took her training wheels off. Since she claimed not to be very religious, she may not have read the high priestly prayer, but the things she said sounded a lot like some of the things Jesus prayed.

"My mother gave so much to me. It is the least I can do to give her comfort and joy," she said. "This brings me joy too," she added. That sounds a lot like glorifying and being glorified, doesn't it?

This self-styled, non-religious person continued, "I just want what is best for her." That sounds a lot like letting go and facing risk and pain with nothing but the strength of love, doesn't it?

When we pray like Jesus, we reach down into the deepest and truest parts of our selves. We acknowledge all the gifts that we have been given. We entrust all whom we hold dear into God's loving care. We recognize that we are not in control. We do not pray for avoidance. We pray for perseverance.

In short, we pray for a story with God that includes the strength and courage to face the inevitable risks and pains. We are living a story with God that involves working through our fears and doubts. We are trusting a story with God in which we are able, even if unwilling, to be pushed beyond our hesitations and uncertainties.

At some point, living with God means the training wheels have to come off so we can discover for ourselves what it means to ride like the wind. At some point, living with God means the wings we have been given must be spread wide so we can experience for ourselves what it means to soar with perfect freedom. At some point, living with God means letting go of the fear and anxiety so we can grow up to become the special, loving apostles whom God has created us to be.

This is our prayer when the time comes for us to be sent out. It is based upon Jesus' prayer before he sent out his very first apostles. By God's grace, we are able to face the risks and pains before us. By God's grace, we do not have to face them alone. Jesus said, "Remember, I am with you always, to the end of the age."

So be not afraid, for we have the gift of God's love by our side. We have been nourished with the very special gifts of communion that make life possible and bearable when the inevitable time comes to take the training wheels off.

Reflecting on Our Story with God

❖ Reflect on how you might find comfort from Jesus' prayer when it is time to remove the training wheels—for ourselves or those we love.

❖ Consider how prayer helps us not to shrink when it is time to face risks and admit that we are not in control.

Celebrating Our Story with God

❖ Think about the parts of your life in which a little more risk might be appropriate. In what ways could you "ride like the wind" or spread your wings or live more deeply into the person God created you to be?

❖ Express your gratitude in a written note to someone who pushed you to take chances that involved some falling, but—in hindsight—were necessary risks to grow and develop.

Afterword

I hope you feel more fortified to take the next step on your pathway and imagine the next chapter in your love story with God and your neighbors. You have the map and the experience to make this journey. I have shared some of the scriptures and stories that have helped me discover deeper meaning in the Holy Eucharist. I encourage you to discover your own favorite scriptures and stories that hold meaning for you and then bring those gifts into your prayer life—both personally and in community with others where you celebrate the Holy Eucharist.

Our sacred stories—ancient and contemporary—fortify us for the journey. They become safe places along the way to share the blessings of life and endure its challenges. Our stories also inspire us in the way of Jesus as we share his faith, hope, and love with others.

We all have a hunger for meaning in this life, and the Holy Eucharist can serve as a vital source of nourishment. Adopted by grace, we are enabled to listen for the mysterious presence and wisdom of God stirring around us.

In spite of our uncertainties, we are nonetheless entrusted to offer our prayers and power as sisters and brothers alongside Christ, the pioneer of this risky faith. We give thanks and remember the words and deeds of Jesus—not only from the past but also in the present since we are still living members of his Body, the Church.

Taste and see that the Lord is good. Receive the strength and courage you need to glorify God by becoming a blessing yourself. After all, you are what you eat. Then take the training wheels off, even though bumps and bruises are inevitable. You are as ready as any apostle ever was to take the next step on your journey.

Acknowledgments

I would like to acknowledge and thank some of the many important teachers and fellow clergy who have helped me explore the depth and mystery of the Holy Eucharist: Jim Turrell, Julia Gatta, Christopher Bryan, Richard Smith, Tom Ward, Bill Stafford, Don Armentrout (deceased), and Marion Hatchett (deceased). I am also grateful for the parochial priests who have been, and continue to be, important role models for me as a rector: Jim Abbott, Michael Bullock, Sally Johnston, and Tom Macfie.

The people of St. Martin's-in-the-Fields Episcopal Church in Columbia, South Carolina, and St. Peter's Episcopal Church in Greenville, South Carolina, have celebrated Holy Eucharist with me for years. I am thankful to have been shaped by these people as well as these prayers.

Finally, I want to thank those who have encouraged and improved this book—Richelle Thompson, Alice Baird, Matt Matthews, Marie Cope, and Kim Buchanan.

Endnotes

[i] This story can be found in 1 Kings 19:8-16.

[ii] The term "plenteous redemption" is drawn from Psalm 130.

[iii] This phrase is drawn from St. Paul's second Letter to the Corinthians, chapter 4.

[iv] This hymn is reprinted with permission by Hope Publishing Company. It can be found in The Hymnal 1982, #597.

[v] *The Book of Common Prayer*, p. 304.

[vi] This phrase comes from the Nicene Creed to express the fullness of Jesus' Divinity.

[vii] This closing sentence from the Service of Morning Prayer comes from Paul's Letter to the Ephesians 3:20.

[viii] The Baptismal Covenant is found on pages 304-305 of *The Book of Common Prayer.*

[ix] These words are drawn from the post-communion thanksgiving prayer from the Holy Eucharist, Rite II, *The Book of Common Prayer,* p. 366.

[x] *The Book of Common Prayer*, p. 219

[xi] Adapted into first person plural from the Presentation of the Sacramental Gifts in the Holy Eucharist, *The Book of Common Prayer*, p. 365.

xii P.F.H. How, A.K.C., Chaplain of Runwell Hospital, Essex, *Aspects of the Eucharist or The Holy Sacrifice*. (Booklet, School of Theology Library, Sewanee, TN).

xiii Our acclamation is inspired by the songs of praise and blessing found in the Revelation to John, including those in chapters 4, 5 and 7.

xiv The Greek word *parakletos* is transliterated into English as "paraclete."

xv These two stories immediately precede the Lord's Prayer. See Luke 10:29-42

xvi Marion Hatchett, *Commentary on the American Prayer Book* (Harper San Francisco, 1995), p. 378.

xvii The Synoptic Gospels all place this story of Jesus' disruption of the temple merchants at the end of his ministry after his triumphal entry into Jerusalem. John's Gospel, on the other hand, places it at the very beginning of Jesus' ministry.

xviii Philip Yancey, *The Jesus I Never Knew*, (Grand Rapids, MI: Zondervan, 1995), p. 13.

xix Philip Yancey, *The Jesus I Never Knew*, p. 15.

xx This reference in John's Gospel is drawn from Psalm 69:9.

xxi Mark 6:52

xxii Ephesians 4:26-5:2

xxiii This translation of Ephesians 5:2 is included in the list of offertory sentences in *The Book of Common Prayer*, p. 376.

xxiv The Greek word in this passage is recorded in the present, continuous tense.

xxv Moses' teaching in Deuteronomy 8:10 refers specifically to "the good land." I substituted "everything" to make this passage clearer to our present context since we don't calculate our blessings in terms of land grants. For the ancient Israelites, "the good land" literally did mean everything to them.

xxvi *The Book of Common Prayer*, p. 366.

xxvii *The Book of Common Prayer*, p. 365.

xxviii Matthew 28:17.

About the Author

Furman L. Buchanan is the rector of St. Peter's Episcopal Church, a growing congregation focused on celebrating, discovering, and sharing the gifts of God through worship, learning, and compassionate service and care. He and his wife, Kim, live in Greenville, South Carolina. They are the parents of three daughters.

About Forward Movement

Forward Movement is committed to inspiring disciples and empowering evangelists. Our ministry is lived out by creating resources such as books, small-group studies, apps, and conferences.

Our daily devotional, *Forward Day by Day*, is also available in Spanish (*Adelante Día a Día*) and Braille, online, as a podcast, and as an app for smartphones or tablets. It is mailed to more than fifty countries, and we donate nearly 30,000 copies each quarter to prisons, hospitals, and nursing homes.

We actively seek partners across the church and look for ways to provide resources that inspire and challenge. A ministry of the Episcopal Church for over eighty years, Forward Movement is a nonprofit organization funded by sales of resources and by gifts from generous donors.

To learn more about Forward Movement and our resources, visit www.ForwardMovement.org. We are delighted to be doing this work and invite your prayers and support.